One Day You'll Thank Me

One Day You'll Thank Me

ESSAYS ON DATING, MOTHERHOOD, AND EVERYTHING IN BETWEEN

CAMERAN EUBANKS WIMBERLY

with Michele Bender

Gallery Books

New York London Toronto Sydney New Delhi

Gallery Books
An Imprint of Simon & Schuster, Inc.
1230 Avenue of the Americas
New York, NY 10020

First Gallery Books trade paperback edition June 2022

GALLERY BOOKS and colophon are registered trademarks of Simon & Schuster, Inc.

For information about special discounts for bulk purchases, please contact Simon & Schuster Special Sales at 1-866-506-1949 or business@simonandschuster.com.

The Simon & Schuster Speakers Bureau can bring authors to your live event. For more information or to book an event, contact the Simon & Schuster Speakers Bureau at 1-866-248-3049 or visit our website at www.simonspeakers.com.

Interior design by Jaime Putorti

Manufactured in the United States of America

10 9 8 7 6 5 4 3 2 1

Library of Congress Cataloging-in-Publication Data
Names: Eubanks Wimberly, Cameran, author.
Title: One day you'll thank me : essays on dating, motherhood, and everything in between / Cameran Eubanks Wimberly ; with Michele Bender.
Description: New York : Gallery Books, 2021. |
Identifiers: LCCN 2020032090 (print) | LCCN 2020032091 (ebook) |
ISBN 9781982150129 (hardcover) | ISBN 9781982150136 (paperback) |
ISBN 9781982150143 (ebook)
Subjects: LCSH: Motherhood. | Dating (Social customs)
Classification: LCC HQ759 .E887 2021 (print) | LCC HQ759 (ebook) |
DDC 306.874/3—dc23
LC record available at https://lccn.loc.gov/2020032090
LC ebook record available at https://lccn.loc.gov/2020032091

ISBN 978-1-9821-5012-9
ISBN 978-1-9821-5013-6 (pbk)
ISBN 978-1-9821-5014-3 (ebook)

This book is dedicated to my mother, Bonnie,
the lighthouse in my life.

When I found out I was pregnant, one of my wise and wonderful best friends, Dru, wrote this to me. I think it's really beautiful, and I'd like to share it with you.

It is a great honor to become a mother. Eckhart Tolle says that parenting is the perfect place to reach enlightenment.

Queen Afua says that Motherhood will make you over if you let it. Yes. She says it will create spiritual, emotional, mental and physical muscle and teach you how to master your own life.

It is all of these things and more.

It is the deepest nirvana ache and the pinnacle of ecstasy.

Listen, this is true: It is the most magnificent fight. It is scratches and balmy tears and milk. It is beautiful, it is bubbly and sweet and defies gravity. It is music: it is jazz and rock and roll, it is old soul and symphony. It is color and sound and light.

Welcome, Sweet Mother Woman.

God bless your new journey, always.

CONTENTS

CONTENTS

INTRODUCTION

If you find it in your heart to care for somebody
else, you will have succeeded.
—MAYA ANGELOU, MOTHER OF ONE

Let me start by saying that nothing brings me more joy than being a mom! Nothing. It's by far the best thing I've ever done and I'm grateful every day for my daughter, Palmer. HOWEVER, motherhood is also by far the hardest thing I have ever done. Ever. Even a few years in, I do not have this whole parenting thing down. Why? Just when you think you've figured out one stage, your child moves on to another.

One reason I wrote this book is because I didn't connect with the flawless parenting images and idyllic moments I saw in the movies and on mommy blogs and Instagram. For me, they could not have been farther from the truth. They made pregnancy and motherhood look magazine perfect, which just makes you feel like you are on the hot mess express. Where was the screaming baby? Where were the dark circles and the hair that hadn't been washed in days? Mom bun, anyone? I once saw a quote attributed to Socrates that said, "What screws us up the most in life is the picture in our head of how it's supposed to be." Amen to that! Sure, I love to post adorable Instagram pics of my daughter, Palmer, in smocked dresses, bows, and cute bathing suits on the beach (dressing a baby girl is so much fun!), but I'm also honest about my pregnancy constipation and less-than-stellar mom-to-be diet, the post-pregnancy pain in my crotch, my fire-hose-like oversupply of breast milk, and my decision to quit breastfeeding just shy of three months, along with Palmer's love affair with her paci (which is really my own inability to take it away from her). Everything, actually.

Why am I oh-so-honest? Maybe giving you TMI on occasion? Because I feel like many, many women don't talk about what you really go through during the first few weeks and months as a new mom. Perhaps it's because they don't want to be labeled as depressed, admit that they didn't have this Instagram-worthy experience or seem like they don't have their shit together. Well, ladies, that's okay. I'm happy to admit it. All of it. In fact, it's normal. I was depressed. My experience wasn't Instagram worthy and no, I didn't have my shit together. (Hardly!) The first week alone was full of sheer exhaustion, shock, lots of tears and not knowing what the hell I was doing. I'm fine sharing this new-mom experience with you because the resounding message that I get every single day from women with newborns is something along the lines of, "Oh my God, I had no idea it was going to be this hard. But then I look at your Instagram and it makes me feel so much better about what I'm going through." I'm also fine shattering the myth that you can have it all. The response has been overwhelming, hence *One Day You'll Thank Me*. I wanted to tell the truth, the whole truth and nothing but the milk-leaking, pee-in-my pants, when-can-I-drop-her-at-day-care truth. But I also wanted to assure you of one thing: you WILL be okay. Or as my mom used to remind me growing up, "This, too, shall pass."

I really believe that timing is everything, including when it comes to having a child. For me, at thirty-five years old I could handle what would have put me into a padded room at twenty-five years old. I also realized that becoming a mom doesn't have to totally rock your world, and just because you have a baby doesn't mean that your life ends; it's just a different life. I was so scared to get pregnant and then even more afraid when I realized that I'm not such a baby person. As a total control freak, the unknown terrifying and let's just say that parenting, no matter how much you read, plan and organize, is lots of unknown. While it's not always easy, what you get back is worth every messy mama moment. Sure, it's full of ups and downs, but you choose how to react to change and you choose your expectations. If you think life as a new parent—or just as a parent at all—is supposed to look neat 'n' tidy, then you'll feel awful that you're not making your own baby food, that you haven't showered in days and that you've become one of those moms whose living room looks like a play-pen. (Yup, that's me. And that's one thing I said I'd never allow. What a snotty bitch I was!) It's important to realize that it kind of sucks at times, but you get through it and it's worth it. Well worth it.

Even though motherhood is tough, tiring and like climbing on a roller coaster every single day, YOU'VE GOT THIS. One thing I'd also say is go with your gut. That is something I've realized along the way as a mother—and in life—because my gut has never failed me. And if you do it all with a sense of humor, you *will* be okay. Trust me: if I can get through it, anyone can! I've survived the first few years of mamahood just fine as a sometimes anxiety-ridden, stressed-out working mom on reality TV who won't hire a nanny. I know it sounds totally sweet and sappy, but you cannot put a price tag on motherhood. It's the best feeling in the entire world just to be loved by your own little child. What I realized is that nobody is perfect; instead, you learn and grow with your baby. Yes, I know that many days I fail as a mom. Sometimes I say bad words, sometimes I let Palmer have a little too much screen time and sometimes I let her watch *The Price Is Right* just so I can drink a warm cup of coffee. Sometimes I cry in front of her. It ain't all roses . . . And guess what? That's all okay! I'm not perfect, but I'm trying, and I sure do love my little girl.

One Day You'll Thank Me

Chapter One

THE REAL WORLD

❧

Seize the moment. Remember all those women on
the *Titanic* who waved off the dessert cart.

—ERMA BOMBECK, MOTHER OF THREE

I have no problem admitting that I was ten times cooler and more fun before I got pregnant and had a child. Today, I may be grandma central and yes, I believe that a perfect night out on the town is a dinner reservation at 5:30 P.M. so that I can be in bed by 8 P.M.—even on my birthday. Actually, *especially* on my birthday. I may have lost my edge and my mojo and have zero social life and I'm totally, 100 percent fine with it. However, real proof that I could hang in my late teens and twenties is the fact that I was on *The Real World* when I was nineteen years old. Here's how it all happened . . .

When I was growing up, there were only four television stations (okay, now I *really* sound like a grandma), and my family

1

didn't get network cable until I was in high school. That is when I started watching *The Real World* on MTV. For those of you who were just a twinkle in your mama's eye at the time, *The Real World* was one of the first reality TV shows. This was long before women were asked to accept this rose on *The Bachelor*, risk takers chose to subsist on rice and just one outfit for thirty-nine days on *Survivor* and, of course, my castmates and I took part in the Charleston social scene on *Southern Charm*. *The Real World* was sort of like *Big Brother*, because total strangers lived together, but it was not a competition, so no one was kicked off and no one won. On *The Real World*, seven total strangers, all from different backgrounds, were picked from across the United States to live in an amazing house and have their lives documented for several months. It was sort of a social experiment. Each season the house was in a different city. The whole concept fascinated me—especially because I'm a country girl who grew up in a small town in upstate South Carolina called Anderson, about three and a half hours from Charleston. My mother grew up there, and so did my mother's mother. Actually, I'm a tenth-generation South Carolinian . . . meaning nobody ever left. Ever. So I always thought it would be really cool to just pick up and move somewhere new to experience something greater/bigger/different. I had no clue that reality TV would offer me that opportunity.

I had always read that the chances of getting on *The Real World* were slim to none. Hundreds of thousands of people applied every year. That said, I still gave it a shot. The summer after my freshman year of college, I saw an ad online that they were currently holding open casting calls around the country for the fourteenth season. I went to MTV's website and found out that Atlanta, Georgia, was one of the cities. *This is only an hour and a half away from me*, I thought. *I should go.* At that time in my life, I had little direction. I had no idea what I wanted to "be" when I got older. I had no burning passion for any one thing and I felt kind of lost. I figured it wouldn't hurt to drive to Atlanta and see what this open casting call was all about. If nothing came of it, at least I could say I auditioned for *The Real World.* At the time, I had no idea which city the show would be in if I *did* get chosen. But my family never really traveled when I was growing up, so the chance to just pick up and move to *anywhere* in the country was part of the allure.

I actually had to forgo my younger sister Cayce's high school graduation to go to the casting call. We are only fifteen months apart and had spent much of our childhood beating the living shit out of each other. But I love her like no other and felt really bad. Although she didn't actually care whether I came to her graduation or not, it ticked my parents off and I got a lot of grief from them about it. Still, I couldn't shake the pull to go to Atlanta and see what would happen next. It sounds crazy, but at the time I had this weird gut feeling that the audition was something that I was supposed to do and that if I did it, against all the crazy odds, I would get picked for the show. As you'll see in this book, my gut never fails me.

So I got dressed (I just wore what I normally did: a short blue jean skirt and white polo top. Very simple. Nothing in your face.) and drove the hour and a half to Atlanta. When I got to the convention center where the casting call was taking place, there was a seemingly endless line wrapped around the building. Some people were in tents and had actually camped out the night before just to get a good place in line. I had absolutely NO idea that it would be this crowded. *Oh my God*, I thought. *This is NUTS*. I considered turning around and going home, but I still couldn't shake this weird feeling that I was supposed to audition. So I got in line and waited. And waited and waited and waited. I'm not sure how long I stood there, but it was hours and hours. When my time finally came, I went inside and was directed to go sit at a table with about seven other people. The casting directors from MTV told us to just talk amongst ourselves and interact with each other. They wanted to see our personalities and how we dealt with other people. It lasted about ten minutes. And that was it. Yes, I'd missed my sister's high school graduation, driven sixty miles, and waited for hours in line, all for ten minutes. Then I got in my car and drove sixty miles home.

About a week later, my phone rang while I was folding laundry. It was a woman from the casting department at MTV.

"Cameran, you've made it to the next stage of the casting process for *The Real World*," she said. "Now we would like to interview you." What happened over the next several months was a very intense interview/screening process to advance through the respective rounds. I had to fill out a questionnaire that was the size of a book. They asked about everything from my belief systems to my family to things that I had done or experienced. On top of that, there were personality profile tests and questions to determine how

I would react to various situations. I also had to travel to two differ-ent cities—one was Jacksonville, Florida, and the other one I can't remember—to conduct more in-person interviews. At one point during one of the interviews, they asked me about my mom. I was talking about all the ways she had been instrumental in helping me develop confidence and self-worth and all the wisdom she imparted to me. It was the first time I had actually talked to someone about it and said these things out loud. Realizing all she had done for me really moved me and I started crying in the interview—not tears of sadness, but of gratitude that I had such a wonderful mother. Soon thereafter, MTV called my family members and friends to get even more information about me. And that's not all. I was also questioned and screened by a psychiatrist. I remember thinking that if I wasn't picked, at least the interview process itself had been an interesting, memorable experience that taught me a lot about myself.

And then it happened! I can remember the moment I got the call as clear as day. "Cameran, congratulations . . . you will be one of the seven strangers on season fourteen of *The Real World*," said Jonathan Murray. He was one of the creators of the show and I could not believe that he was on the other end of the phone. "We'll be filming in San Diego. Get ready to leave in two weeks." *Oh my gosh!* I thought. *I'm leaving South Carolina and going to California.* I felt like I was on a cloud. If there was one place I wished to go in this country, it was Southern California. I had been there twice as a child to visit my aunt and uncle who lived in Orange County. Ever since then, the Golden State seemed like a dream to me: always sunny, always warm. Palm trees everywhere and just a completely different vibe than I was used to growing up in a small town in the Deep South. The news that I was about to live there for five months was probably the most exciting thing to ever happen in my life at that point. I couldn't pack my bags fast enough.

I called my mom immediately. "This is a very pivotal decision for you," she said after I told her. "Especially at such a young age." My mom was never a controlling parent, so she didn't tell me it was the right or wrong thing to do. Instead, as always, she said she would support my decision but to be very careful about the way I carried myself while filming the show. "This could end up being a very good thing or a very bad thing, and that will be based solely on the decisions you make," she added. Besides my mom and other close family members, MTV said I wasn't allowed to tell anyone about the show. They didn't want me or any other cast members mentioning *The Real World*, so if people asked where I was going, I was supposed to say "to film a documentary." Luckily, no one asked. I mean, c'mon, who would believe I was going to film a documentary? On what? I couldn't scream about *The Real World* from the rafters but, y'all, I was SO, SO excited. My family was supportive, but a little hesitant about what I was about to do . . . after all, I was only nineteen years old and pretty naive. Looking back, I believe this is actually why I was chosen. Going into the casting process, I think the producers knew they were looking for one of the personalities to be a small-town Southern girl who was as naive as they come. I fit the bill perfectly.

MTV told me that pretty much everything I needed would be provided other than my own personal clothing. "Make sure to bring 'going out' clothes," they said. *Um, what?* I didn't own anything even *remotely* sophisticated or "hip" to wear to nightclubs in California. So my dad took me to Bebe at a local mall and bought me two black dresses. I swear I felt like Cinderella (in an odd way). Even though I had only two weeks to get ready to leave for five months, I was a nineteen-year-old college student who didn't own much, so it wasn't like I had to scramble to pack it all up or get it organized. Instead, it felt like I was just resetting my life, and it felt good. So off I went to California with just one big suitcase.

The first time I walked into the *Real World* house in San Diego, a big, bright blue modern house that sat on the end of a fishing wharf, it felt like I was walking into a celebrity's home. It was so different from anything I had ever seen or lived in in South Carolina. It had three bedrooms—the guys shared one, the girls the other two—lots of decks and a hot tub. The decor was all very brightly colored and young/hip, with a definite beach/surfer theme to go along with the Southern California location. I couldn't believe this was going to be my home for five months.

The show was filmed from August to December, and then would premiere the following January with twenty-six episodes. There were seven of us in our house—four girls and three boys. Here's how they described me and my housemates: Southern belle Cameran, 19; motorcycle enthusiast Brad, 22; certified masseuse Frankie, 21; quick-witted Jacquese, 19; San Francisco native Jamie, 20; Randy, 24, who worked at a Boston nightclub; and Robin, 22, a bartender in Tampa. When I met my new roommates for the first time, I instantly loved them all. Although most *Real World* casts fight a lot, we genuinely liked each other and had a good time together. Our cast had a unique bond. I immediately had a crush on Brad. As a motorcycle-loving boy from Chicago, he was *nothing* like the guys I was used to in small-town South Carolina. He had a loud mouth, said what he felt and had little decorum. I found him to be very refreshing and interesting! I shared a room with Jamie Chung, a beautiful Korean-American girl from San Francisco who went on to become a successful actress. I was in total awe of her effortless California style—she wore UGG boots before they became a thing. I thought she was just so cool and by the end of our stay, I was definitely copying every single thing she wore. Jamie and I keep in touch to this day.

The number-one question I get about *The Real World* is, "What's it like to be filmed 24/7?" Well, let's just say that the minute we set foot in the house on day one, a microphone pack was put on our backs and our every move and sound was recorded and logged all day, every day, for five months. The microphone packs were hot and uncomfortable—something I never really got used to—and you could only remove them to shower or sleep. But you still didn't get breaks in the bathroom or when you went to sleep. The bedrooms were equipped with motion-sensor night vision cameras and there was a microphone built into the headboard of your bed. If you changed positions while you slept, you could hear the camera mounted over the bed move to follow you. It didn't make for very restful sleep. Then there was the bathroom. If you were talking in the shower, a camera and sound guy would come over with a boom to capture what you were saying. Even a menial task such as taking the garbage out involved a camera crew following you. It was *so* different from what I would later experience while filming *Southern Charm*, which we shot just three or four days a week for several hours at a time. Sure, it was weird being filmed 24/7 for the first few days, but the odd thing was . . . I got very used to it, and then it became my new normal. So much so that we were actually offered therapy once we wrapped the show to help us deal with transitioning back to the actual real world from *The Real World*. I guess when your every move is filmed, it can be a little psychologically difficult to return to normal afterward.

The one thing I *never* got used to, however, was the community shower. We had one BIG shower with five showerheads and zero privacy. I could not fathom showering with any of my roommates or them seeing me naked. I also could not imagine the camera crew filming me naked. My solution was to take all of my showers wearing a bikini. We also had a very small closet in the basement of the house that I would sneak off to so I could get dressed in private. I was *such* a prude. However, I can proudly say that no editor on MTV had to blur my naked behind! I think this made my mother proud.

Each season of *The Real World*, the cast gets a group job while filming the show. Rumor had it that we were originally intended to work at SeaWorld, but something changed last minute and the producers had to scramble to find us another job. We ended up being hired as the co-crew for an America's Cup sailing yacht named *Stars and Stripes* and worked about four days a week for a large portion of the day. It always felt like very long hours and we were always really, really tired when we finished. *Stars and Stripes* was a massive vessel that was docked in the San Diego harbor and took tourists out sailing every day. We had to undergo strict training to learn how to safely help crew the ship. For the most part, we loathed the job. It was pretty labor intensive and repetitive. You also had to be on high alert, because there was an element of danger to it. We were told to pay very close attention when changing the sails, as a mishap could cost us a limb. Looking back, though, those days on the boat were some of my best. We learned teamwork and how to push through something we didn't enjoy. We learned what a hard day's work was at a young age. And of course, returning to the harbor on that boat witnessing a SoCal sunset was a very good end to a hard day and made for some amazing memories.

The Real World opened my eyes to so much and I truly think helped shape who I am as a person. It showed me a world beyond the somewhat sheltered Southern culture that I grew up with. It allowed me to live with and learn to get along with a very diverse group of people who had different beliefs and backgrounds. It taught me how to respect all people regardless of their station or circumstance in life. It also showed me how truly naive I was. I had never witnessed anyone using any drugs besides marijuana in South Carolina. But in California I saw cocaine for the first time one night at a club in downtown San Diego. A beautiful girl was snorting it on the counter in the women's bathroom and I watched her in total shock. This was something I thought people only did in movies or on street corners.

"Oh my God. What are you doing?!" I said. I'm certain that my mouth was hanging wide open.

"F*** off," she told me as she looked up with a stare that pierced right through me. Shell-shocked, I immediately started crying. I went out and told all my roommates what I had just witnessed, and they just rolled their eyes and laughed. So I'm not joking when I say I was naive.

At nineteen years old, I was the baby of our group and had to use a fake ID to get into bars and clubs. Being underage and not very streetwise, I could be somewhat of a buzzkill to my roommates. One night, Brad and Robin both got arrested (for different things) and it was crazy. It was the first time I had ever known anyone who was arrested. The thought of them sitting in a jail cell horrified me, especially Robin. Brad got thrown in the drunk tank for being belligerent, but Robin was arrested and booked on an assault charge that was the result of defending *me*. We had been trying to get me into a bar with my fake ID. A guy was heckling us, so Robin punched him in the arm. I can't remember exactly what he was saying, but he was making fun of me for having to use a fake ID and getting caught by the bouncer. I think if there hadn't been cameras around it wouldn't have been an issue, but it was all captured on film. I felt really bad that she was arrested. As you might imagine, we were not welcomed with open arms by some people in San Diego. People would heckle us nonstop when we went to public places. Attempts by people to start fights and provoke us were not uncommon. On numerous occasions, we had to have security follow us to protect the crew's very expensive equipment.

After *The Real World* aired, my friends and family were very supportive. For the most part, I had behaved and didn't cause any serious embarrassment to my family. I didn't have sex with anyone or get in any fights. I was pretty much just myself throughout the duration of filming and although my naiveté was quite apparent, I made it through the process unscathed. The most intriguing/risqué thing I did was have a steamy make-out session in the hot tub with Brad—twice. Of course, the cameras caught us both times. I was absolutely wasted and I'm pretty sure he was, too. The Southern belle had a crush on the bad boy from Chicago! I'm sure this is what the producers were hoping for when they cast us. When we finally gave in to our primal urges and made out, I know they were high-fiving each other in the control room. It never evolved into deep feelings, though, and Brad never tried anything else. In fact, Brad and I traveled together extensively after the show for speaking engagements about *The Real World* and even stayed in the same hotel room on numerous occasions . . . but we always had separate beds. I still think of him as a dear friend. In fact, I went to his wedding in Chicago years ago. I'm also in touch with Randy and Jamie. We have talked about trying to arrange a roommates' reunion, because we'd love to see each other again. Sadly, Frankie passed away several years ago from her lifelong battle with cystic fibrosis.

After *The Real World*, I had many amazing, unique, and sometimes crazy opportunities presented to me. It was hard to go back to school when I still had no idea what I wanted to do with my life and when I was being offered jobs and money that were so hard to pass up. In a matter of weeks, I went from being a completely private/unknown person to somewhat of a celebrity. I HATE to use the word *celebrity* because, to me, the only people who deserve that title are those who have done something noteworthy . . . but all of a sudden people knew who I was. I would go to the mall and people would ask for my picture. It was kind of cool and kind of terrifying at the same time. This was in the heyday of *The Real World* and people were truly fascinated by the concept, so for the two years following the show I went on a speaking circuit to over fifty colleges and universities, from Duke to UCLA. There was rarely an empty seat in the house. Between the speaking engagements, we would do appearances at bars and clubs and get paid in wads of cash. We would literally stand on top of the bar with a handle of alcohol and pour it into people's mouths. The club appearances typically lasted until about two in the morning.

One of the, um, craziest opportunities was hosting *Girls Gone Wild*, a series of videos of college-aged girls going, well, wild—and not being shy about flashing their boobs or other areas of their bodies and taking part in wet T-shirt contests. Occasionally Joe Francis, the founder of *Girls Gone Wild*, would have celebrities on the show, and he had the idea to have a small group of people from *The Real World* host an episode. At the time, I thought the extent of *Girls Gone Wild* was just girls flashing their boobs. I had NO idea it was pretty much soft-core porn. Joe offered us each $10,000 to get on the bus for two days and film. I said yes. *This could be fun and it's easy money*, I thought. Well, I was in shock by the whole thing. Mildly fascinated, but mostly in total shock. The fact that people were willing to have sex on camera floored me. I was mortified. I ended up crying and begging the girls not to take off their clothes—not exactly the role of the host. In fact, I think that was the exact opposite of my job. File this one under "you live, you learn." I will try to avoid telling Palmer about the adventure.

I was on a plane almost every week and sometimes multiple times a week. I would fly to the East Coast to speak at a college one day, and the following day I would have to be on the West Coast. I made a ton of money doing this and also blew a ton of money doing it. This was the first time in my life that I had a lot of money, but I had nobody helping me manage it. If I went out to dinner with friends, I would pick up the whole bill. I bought a white Cadillac Escalade. I had a Juicy Couture tracksuit in every color. I thought I was hot stuff, but looking back, I was kind of a moron. Knowing what I do now as a mature adult, if I had saved and invested that money, it could have really grown. It was an exciting yet difficult time in my life. At the end of it, I got very sick and burned out. I went to see a doctor who told me, "Cameran, you have to stop all of this traveling. You are physically exhausted and it's affecting your health." He was right. The constant flying, drinking, lack of sleep and eating airport food had caught up to me. (This is part of the reason why I made a rule for myself, when I decided to do *Southern Charm*, to stick to a two-drink maximum while filming. I'm a lightweight, and you really get in trouble when you let your guard down when you're shit-faced.) It was time for something new.

That's when I got hired by the NFL network to be a correspondent for Rich Eisen's *NFL Total Access*. To this day, a lot of people have no idea I did this, but it had always been a dream of mine to work on the sidelines of a football field, and I jumped at the opportunity when it fell in my lap. I'm pretty sure Rich was mortified that a girl just coming off *The Real World* had been hired to work on a show that he'd put a lot of time and expertise into. I had a contract for ten NFL games, and my segment was titled "Behind the Scenes with Cameran Eubanks," where I showed viewers what was happening at the game besides the game. I was told that I needed to tone down my thick Southern accent a bit before I started, so I would listen to newscasters and try to learn ways to sound not so "country."

But my accent wasn't the only problem. I was absolutely awful at this new job! I was totally, 100 percent green. As green as you could be. It was mind-blowingly exciting to me, but I had ABSO-LUTELY no idea what I was doing. I interviewed tons of celebrities, including John Legend, Mary J. Blige and Warren Moon. I stood inside the tunnel at Lambeau Field with Brett Favre. I went inside the Patriots' locker room and tried on Tom Brady's shoulder pads. At the NFL kickoff game in New York, I interviewed Beyoncé. Yes, Beyoncé. She actually told me she watched our season of *The Real World* and was a huge fan. *Wait, what?* I thought. I was shaking so much that the microphone was moving when I talked to her. If you think I'm lying, I have the awful and embarrassing video footage to prove it. The whole time I was filming that show, I thought, *I can't believe I'm doing this. Whoever hired me is probably gonna get fired.* When Elton John was at one of the games, I was handed a microphone by my producer and told, "Get to Elton!" I literally couldn't do it. I was too terrified. Y'all, this job was not for me. I sucked. Needless to say, my contract was not renewed . . . and I totally understood why. Looking back, I think I lacked the confidence to be good at something like this. It just felt so far out of reach for me. I also felt guilty that some people work their whole lives and go to school for an opportunity like this, and I got it only because I had just come off *The Real World.*

I used to say that I hope Palmer never finds out about *The Real World* because obviously there were some embarrassing things I don't want her to see. (For example, the hot tub sessions with Brad.) But now I view it differently. It was a great learning experience and it played a big role in my generation's pop culture, so I'm proud to have been a part of it. I'll probably let her watch some of it once she's about sixteen years old, and who knows, she might even think it's cool. Now, if Palmer wanted to do a show similar to *The Real World* the way reality TV was done back then, I would support it. Sadly, I can't say the same about supporting her to do reality TV the way it is done now. As a culture, I feel like it takes a lot to shock us these days. We are numb to so much because of social media. We all want to see drama for entertainment, but the drama that it now takes to sustain a good reality TV show has become a little too dark and too manufactured. It also comes at the expense of the participants who are filmed. Another reason I wouldn't want her to do it today: social media did not exist when we filmed *The Real World.* There were online message boards and chat rooms, but that was it. I have a MUCH thicker skin in my thirties than I did when I was nineteen. Social media back in the day would have chewed me up and spit me out.

People always ask me: if I could turn back time, would I go back and do *The Real World* again? I always answer with an emphatic yes, yes, YES. That experience was a major turning point in my life. It helped shape me as a person and opened my eyes to so much. I would 100 percent go back and do it all over again. There is nothing scarier than going outside of your comfort zone, but when you do you often learn, see and experience things you never imagined. So if an opportunity comes your way—be it reality TV, a new job, a chance to move to a different city, etc.—I'd say, grab it. Chances are, it will grow you as a person, and that's what life is all about.

Chapter Two

HOW DATING ALL THE WRONG GUYS LED ME TO THE RIGHT ONE

Someday, someone will walk into your life and make
you realize why it never worked with anyone else.

—SHON MEHTA

I may be a tenth-generation South Carolinian, but I was definitely NOT one of those Southern women whose whole life revolved around getting married and having the house, the white picket fence and two children (preferably one boy and one girl). My parents did not have a good marriage. They separated when I was eight years old and divorced when I was fifteen. It was very hard for my sister and me to go through, so when I was young I made a pact with myself: never enter a marriage that I had an inkling of doubt about. I knew that I'd be JUST FINE if I wasn't married with a child by my thirties. Life would go on. To me, never getting married was definitely better than being unhappy. And having a child wasn't a must.

In my twenties, I had quite the dating life. My first serious relationship started at twenty-one with a guy I met in Cancún, Mexico, of all places. After *The Real World,* MTV hired me to go down to Cancún for a month and host spring break parties with several other cast members. Looking back, I'm not sure how I survived that month! The guy I met was on vacation with friends. He was a professional athlete, and I ended up getting engaged to him three years later, at the age of twenty-four. This relationship taught me so much and I remain grateful for it, but we were just not compatible. At that point in his life, he was at the height of his sports career and training for the Olympics, so he needed a copilot and I was not able to be that for him. He needed someone who was flexible and willing to put some of her own needs aside so he could manage his very hectic schedule. I was young and had my own dreams and missed my family. It made me very resentful to have to follow him around the country, and that just wasn't a recipe for a strong relationship. I think he proposed to me because he felt like he needed to, and as it was happening, I knew a wedding would never come to fruition. We broke up a few months after we got engaged. For me this was a lesson learned: timing is everything when it comes to solid relationships. You can love a person with all your heart, but if the timing is off, it just won't work.

Looking back now, it was crazy of me to even think of getting married at twenty-four years old. Yes, some people get lucky and marry their high school sweetheart and live happily ever after. But I feel like that's very rare, and I hear fewer and fewer of those stories the older I get. In my opinion, the twenties are a time for growth and for figuring out who YOU are and what YOU want. What can you live with? And what can you live without? What are the total deal breakers in a partner? The nonnegotiables? And what are the must-haves? I had no idea what I wanted in myself at the age of twenty-four, much less what I wanted in someone I planned to spend the rest of my life with. I think the best way to figure this out is to date, date, date . . . and, well, break up a few times, too. Those who get it right on the first try are just lucky. So in my twenties I tried to say yes to most date offers because it was almost like research. I told myself that if I saw a red flag in any guy I was dating, I had to move on and not make excuses for him. You can love somebody all you want, but if you realize you just aren't compatible on fundamental things, it is probably time to move on. I wanted to get engaged only one more time.

When I was twenty-eight years old, I moved back to Charleston from Annapolis, Maryland, after another failed relationship. (Hello, Cameran, stop moving for men!) This relationship failed because I couldn't trust the guy. He was wonderful in all other areas and we got along great, but he gave me some reasons to not trust him fully that I could never get past. I'm a firm believer that if someone is capable of cheating on you once, they can and probably will do it again . . . especially if you forgive them. Again . . . red flag. BIG one. I was determined to hold out hope that I could meet a man who I would never have to question. (Life will keep repeating the same lessons until you learn from them. Truest thing I know!) But as you can imagine, at this point when I moved back to Charleston, I was over guys, y'all. It seemed like everyone I dated had let me down in some capacity and I just wanted to be single, solo, on my own. Or at least that was the plan. Of course, we all know what happens when you make plans. God laughs and mixes things up a bit. Literally a week after that breakup and my move to Charleston, I got a call from my friend Mona.

"Cam, there's a guy you *have* to meet," she said. Mona was a Realtor and this guy was one of her clients.

"Thanks, but no thanks," I said. "I'm sick of men right now and don't want to date anyone for a while. A long while."

"I know. I know. I get it. But this guy is one in a million. I promise," Mona insisted. *Sure, that's what they all say*, I thought.

"No thanks," I repeated.

But Mona pushed and pushed, so I finally agreed to meet Mr. One in a Million—begrudgingly. Yes, I was still over men and, yes, I was still going to stick to my plan to be solo for a long time. I was ONLY agreeing to go out with the guy because I thought a lot of my friend and if I could trust anyone to set me up on a blind date, it was Mona. Her guy's name was Jason, and he and I made plans to have dinner on Sullivan's Island, a small beach town about twenty minutes from downtown Charleston. It has several cute, no-frills restaurants and is a great spot for a first date. His idea, not mine. The morning of the date I woke up with a pit in my stomach, feeling like it was a big mistake. *I'm not ready. I just DON'T want to date anyone*, I thought. As strange as this may sound, I'd actually never been on a blind date, so by the time 6 P.M. came around, my stomach was in knots and I was sweating. I was dreading the awkward small talk that comes when you meet someone for the first time or—even worse—the painful moments of silence that can linger when you have nothing to say. *Good Lord! What the heck am I doing?* Also, my date was nine years older than me, which seemed like a lot at the time, and a doctor. *He's probably a huge nerd and will be* way *too serious*, I thought as I did my hair and makeup. I also contemplated the fact that this guy was a doctor. *He may be a nerd, but he's* done *something with his life. My biggest accomplishment so far is being on MTV! Is that even an accomplishment? Oh my God, what will we have in common? Probably not one thing.* Still, I forced myself to get dressed, get in my car and go.

You drive from Charleston to Sullivan's Island by taking the Ben Sawyer Bridge, a swing bridge that connects the town of Mount Pleasant with the island. When I got there, the bridge was in the process of opening to let a sailboat through, and traffic came to a complete halt for a good fifteen minutes. *Maybe this is a sign that I should turn around*, I wondered. I even thought about calling my date and faking a migraine to get out of it. But for some reason, I didn't, and I'm so glad.

Jason and I first saw each other in the parking lot while getting out of our cars and right off the bat, I could tell that he was SO different from anyone I had ever dated in the past. He was subdued, calm, collected and soft-spoken, with zero ego. Yet he was very sure of himself. He seemed super genuine and looked me right in the eye when talking. I felt an immediate ease around him. Unlike so many guys, he spoke very little of himself on our first date and instead asked a lot about me. There was not one ounce of him that I felt was trying to show off in any way. It was very refreshing. I could tell he was intrigued by me and wanted to get to know me, not just get into my pants. I felt like I was on a date with a REAL MAN for the first time. All in all, despite my nerves and worries and the fact that we were total opposites, the date went very well. At one point, I reached over with my fork to taste something on his plate. He later told me he was shocked I did that on a first date, but it shows that I somehow felt comfortable enough with him to, well, not use my best manners. Luckily, he wasn't turned off.

"I'd like to see you again," Jason said, very directly, as he walked me to my car. *No games. Wow*, I thought. *This is a first.*

"Okay, sure," I said.

I was very happy as I drove home, but I also didn't feel any immediate chemistry, something I'd always thought was super important. Still, in my gut I liked this guy. A couple of days later he called while I was driving.

"I know this might be a little much for a second date, but I have two tickets to see Prince in concert. Would you like to go?" *UM, PRINCE? . . . YES!!!* I couldn't answer him fast enough. It was on that date that I knew I was going to marry this man. He let his guard down a bit and I got to see his humorous side. The chemistry started kicking in. Now I really wanted to go on a third date. And, well, the rest is history.

It was definitely a whirlwind romance. Jason was and is so different from the macho, egocentric guys I'd always dated. Jason was the first guy who was a complete gentleman with me. He was always respectful . . . almost to a fault. He didn't even try to kiss me until our fifth date! He is confident without being cocky. He is also very warmhearted and super laid-back. And very, very important to me both at the time and now is that Jason is the most sincere and faithful human I know. He rarely gets rattled, so if shit is going down, he is the person that you want in the room. In fact, he has raised his voice at me only one time in nine years. It was back when we were dating. We were on his boat and got caught in some very rough water. I was totally freaking out, pacing back and forth, screaming, "OMG. WE ARE GONNA DIE," grabbing life jackets and acting like a total fool. Of course, Jason was trying to stay calm so he could concentrate and steer the boat. I wouldn't shut up, and my frenetic energy wasn't helping the situation in the least. He finally looked at me and said very loudly, "You need to be quiet and sit the f*** down." Guess what? I got real quiet and sat the f*** down. But you know what else is different about Jason? How I knew he was THE one? Jason has never said anything even remotely negative to me, not even in a teasing way. Some guys I had dated would say little demeaning things to me that weren't outright mean, but still made me feel insecure. Looking back, I realize they did this because *they* were the ones who were insecure. A good man who is secure in himself won't ever demean you, and Jason has never, EVER put me down. Ever. Not even in the slightest way. Now, let me tell you, that's when you KNOW you have a good man. (I also know I got a good one because he's never *once* complained about my side of the bathroom or the fact that I hoard makeup and beauty products, and trust me, I've got a lot of them.) And I was totally wrong about doctors being nerds. Sure, doctors are married to their profession in a lot of ways (Jason will work forty-eight hours straight some weekends), but the flip side of the coin is that they are typically very committed and solid individuals.

People often ask me what Jason initially thought of my having been on *The Real World,* but he had never even seen the show. After all, when it aired, he was in the middle of medical school—clearly, a much more valiant path in life. He knew I was on the show because some people had told him, but to be honest, he never really asked me about it. He also didn't judge me for it. Reality TV has never been on his radar, which may be one of the reasons we get along.

Jason and I dated for three years before we got engaged. Both of our families vacationed at a little beach town called Edisto Island, and that is where he proposed. I wish I could say I was surprised, but here's why I wasn't. The sun was setting and I had just taken a shower. I wasn't wearing any makeup and my hair was soaking wet. Jason came to me and said, "Let's go take a walk on the beach."

"Okay," I said, putting on my flip-flops.

"Well . . . um . . . shouldn't you go fix your hair first?" Unfortunately, nothing gets past me, so my radar was up. *Oh shit,* I thought. *He's gonna propose and doesn't want me to look like I just woke up.* So I dried my hair, put on a little makeup and, sure enough, ten minutes later we were engaged. It was one of the happiest moments of my life.

A week or so later, I had to make one thing clear to Jason. "Just so you know, if kids are a nonnegotiable for you, you can't marry me because I might not give them to you. The last thing I want you to do is resent me or us end up divorced because you want a child and I don't." I had brought this up randomly in conversation while we were dating but wanted to be crystal clear now that we were moving on to the next step in our relationship.

"Cameran, if it happens, it happens. But if not, I love you and want to marry you," Jason said.

When we got married, I was thirty years old, which is considered ancient in the South. In fact, I was one of the last of my group of friends to tie the knot. But I think as you get older you know what you want, and it's definitely worth waiting for the right person. Also, choosing the right partner is paramount when having children, and even though I didn't want children at the time, I knew Jason would be a great father if I ever changed my mind.

I'm fine admitting that the smartest decision I ever made was marrying Jason. We got married in a beautiful outdoor ceremony beneath a large live oak, and I had Mona do a special reading there because I see her as my fairy godmother who brought Jason to me. It was a very Southern wedding. Except for the fact that I chose to walk down the aisle by myself, which is pretty much blasphemy in Southern culture. It just felt odd to me to be "given away." I also knew I wanted both of my parents involved in some way, so they both escorted me arm in arm to the beginning of the aisle and then individually walked down before me. When I saw Jason and started walking, I cried happy tears the whole way down.

I'm not saying Jason is perfect. On our honeymoon we were late for our flight, so Jason ran ahead. HE got on the plane, but I didn't make it, so they closed the door.

"You have to let me on this flight," I told the gate agent, in tears. "This is my honeymoon."

"We're sorry, but it's illegal to open the door once it's closed," she said, shaking her head. After a lot more begging and crying, the gate agent either felt sympathy toward me or wanted me out of her face, so she eventually opened the door. When I saw Jason, I said, "You left me," and the rest of the passengers booed him. Turns out he thought he could hold the plane for me. (He also once bought me a South Carolina lifetime hunting and fishing license as a gift. I'd rather have had a designer bag, but it's the thought that counts, isn't it?)

Besides that, the biggest thing we argue about is Jason's ability to be on time. He is laid-back to a fault. His friends in college called him SoCo (short for Southern Comfort) due to his nonchalant nature. To me, being on time is actually late, and I prefer to be early. I have started MANY fights about this. Out of all the faults one could have, though, it could be much worse. He is a good egg and our married life has been really great. And I think it's been really great, in part, because I chose to keep it off of reality television. People often asked me why Jason was not on *Southern Charm*. They thought it was because he didn't approve of it, but that's not the case. He was actually a big fan and was very good friends with everyone in the cast; in fact, Jason was the one who pushed me to do it every season. He always supported my filming the show even though he wanted no part of the spotlight.

Luckily, Jason was always okay with the fact that I am not a "homemaker" type. Before the wedding, I registered for very expensive Mottahedeh china, and I've served a meal on it *once*. I don't entertain. I don't cook Thanksgiving dinner. I'm pretty useless in the kitchen except for pulling the meat off a rotisserie chicken from the grocery store and pairing it with some premade potato salad from the deli. When I bake cookies, they are the ones you pull apart from frozen dough. I suck at cleaning, too. We don't have any type of cleaning service come to the house because it weirds me out, so I'm the maid . . . and not a very good one. Sometimes I realize our sheets haven't been changed in a month. Oops. Bless Jason's heart, he never complains.

The bottom line when it comes to relationships is to think about the big picture, which is the rest of your life. A good relationship is meeting each other halfway. If one person is always making deposits and the other is always taking, taking, taking, it's a recipe for disaster. Communication and compromise must be the foundations of your relationship. There's a lot of shit I do that I don't want to do to appease my husband and a lot of shit he does that he doesn't want to do to appease me. THAT's called marriage. A book that was a game changer for me relationship-wise was *The 5 Love Languages* by Gary Chapman. The gist is that every person has a love language: Acts of Service, Physical Touch, Quality Time, Words of Affirmation or Receiving Gifts. I am Quality Time and Jason is Acts of Service. Knowing what your partner's love language is and being able to fulfill it is SO important. If you are with someone who doesn't understand what your love language is or, even worse, isn't able to give it to you, then your relationship is not going to be easy. So I can *tell* Jason how much I love him all day long, but he needs to be *shown* that I care. I know this about Jason and try my hardest to *do* things for him like not overreacting to something stupid (which I have a natural tendency to do), helping him with yard work or making him a meal when he has had a long, hard day. These things are not natural for me, but I work to be conscious of them because I love him.

Although it was tough to go through some heartbreak and distrust and guys who just didn't appreciate me, it was well worth all that pain to find Jason. Dating is totally a learning experience, and no relationship is ever a failure if you grow from it. Like the saying goes, "If you wanna get to the castle, you gotta swim the moat."

Chapter Three

SHOULD I OR SHOULDN'T I?
Coming to the Decision to Get Pregnant

It's good to do uncomfortable things.
It's weight training for life.
—ANNE LAMOTT, MOTHER OF ONE

Just because you have a vagina doesn't mean you should pop
out a kid. In fact, a lot of people SHOULDN'T pop them
out, and I thought for most of my life that included me. I admit
it. I could not imagine sitting at home all day with a baby. Honestly, that was my version of hell. I was not one of those little
girls who played with dolls or one of those teenagers who was
babysitting every kid in the neighborhood. In my twenties and
early thirties, the idea of me having a maternal instinct was as
farfetched as me skipping Chick-fil-A for a week. Not happening! Heck, I never had a houseplant that lived longer than four
weeks.

I loved that my twenties and early thirties were all about me, me, me. I knew that if I brought a child into this world I was not going to half-ass it, so I would have to be at a point in my life when I was willing to stop being the center of my own universe. So three years into our marriage, when Jason made it crystal clear that he was ready to be a parent, I wondered: was I?

As I've mentioned, my family has been in South Carolina for ten generations, and growing up in this part of the country, you're taught that you're supposed to want the white picket fence and get married and pregnant in your twenties. (I have childhood friends who have teenagers now.) And you don't have just one kid, you have to have at least two. I don't subscribe to that. In my opinion, parenthood is a choice, not a given, and in my early thirties, I was nowhere near ready to get knocked up. In fact, I was doing everything I could each month *not* to get pregnant. Seeing some of my friends struggle with motherhood reaffirmed my belief that you should only bring a child into this world when you are damn ready for it, when you are aching for it, and there was no ache in my body for a child.

Before we got engaged, I told Jason, "If having a kid is non-negotiable for you, don't marry me." Well, he still married me, and my mind didn't change. That said, Jason is nine years older than me, and it was only a matter of time before he started talking about the pitter-patter of little feet. *Damn*, I thought. I was kind of hoping we could practice for or even stave off a baby with a pup, but no such luck. (In the end, we wound up with a baby AND a dog.) When we'd see a kid doing something like throwing a football with his dad, Jason would say, "That will be so nice," while I'd think, *Kids are assholes.* Not to mention my fear of actually being pregnant! I thought pregnancy was, well, kind of gross and I worried about all the changes that would happen to my body. (Who knew how much I'd love having boobs and hips? At least while pregnant. But more on that later!) Another fear? I was petrified that I couldn't properly carry a baby to term because I'm a small woman. It didn't help when one of Jason's colleagues who is an ob-gyn saw me and said, "Wow . . . you're a textbook C-section. Your hips are way too small to deliver vaginally." *Um . . . thanks?*

Everyone around me was on the Cameran-should-have-a-baby bandwagon. "Do it now. It's the time. You'll be so great," they'd tell me. They'd actually been saying that for years. But since they weren't the ones who'd have to cook the kid for nine months and then push him or her out of their swollen vag, I didn't want to hear their opinions. To an outsider, there was no reason why I shouldn't have a baby. I was happily married, I was financially stable and Jason and I both have loving, supportive families. But I didn't feel like I was equipped for the job.

If Jason hadn't wanted a kid, I wouldn't have had anything to worry about. But he believed in his heart all along that one day I would be ready, too, and the fact that I still wasn't concerned me. *If I never decide to have a child, will Jason resent me?* I wondered. So I had to take a deeper look at what was going on. Was my indecision rooted in the anxiety I've struggled with for most of my life? Or was I simply not maternal? I decided to see a therapist. At our first session, she asked, "When you think of having a child, are you gaining something or giving up something?" OMG. That hit me like a ton of bricks.

"I feel like I'm giving up something," I said. It was the truth. Everybody I talked to said your life changes so much when you have a baby, but I LOVED my life. It was great! Why mess with it? I didn't want things to change. What my anxiety kept me from realizing at the time was that a lot of that change is positive.

"I also feel like having a child is a potential for something to go wrong," I told the therapist.

"So you'll feel like you're not in control?" she asked.

Bingo! She nailed it again. My name is Cam and I'm a control freak. For heaven's sake, y'all, I can't be a passenger in a car unless I really know the driver—actually, I can't be a passenger in a car, period—and when you have a child you are NOT in the driver's seat. You have to totally give up control in your life. Just thinking about that made me sweat.

"Let's put it this way," I told the therapist. "If I found out I was pregnant tomorrow, I would be terrified. I'd think my life was over."

I knew my mother was dying to be a grandmother. God bless her, she'd already saved up an overflowing Ziploc bag of trinkets for that future grandchild—all very small objects that could easily be lodged in a kid's throat, like marbles, coins and McDonald's Happy Meal toys. (I don't think Palmer will be sticking her hand in my mom's bag of choking hazard treasures until she's a teenager.) But despite this, my mom was very supportive when I shared what I'd discussed with the therapist.

"That tells you right there that you're certainly not leaning toward having a child," she said.

"And you don't think that's weird?" I asked.

"Heck no," she said emphatically.

"Everyone I know keeps saying, 'Do it now. You'll be so great.'"

"Honey, there's nothing wrong with people who choose not to have children. My friends who are childless by choice are really happy," she said. "In fact, they are very intelligent and thoughtful. Any fool can have a baby. Don't go by what you feel society is telling you to do. You are the only one who can make up your mind about this." Yup, my mama has always had my back.

"Aren't you having a good time in your life?" she added.

"Yes. I love my life. And without a kid, I'll have more money to put you in a really nice nursing home," I joked.

Whenever I have to make a hard decision, I write a pro/con list. It's something I've been doing since I was a child. So one day I was making a kids-versus-no-kids list when Jason asked what I was doing. When I told him, he also made a list of what he thought our life would be WITH kids and WITHOUT. It was mind-opening to compare my list to his. Jason had written: "With kids, our lives would be enriched, our lives would be more meaningful and our lives would be busier. Without kids, our lives would be lonely, simple and unfulfilled." Wow. That really woke me up. This was something Jason really wanted, something he'd feel empty without. And the truth was, reading Jason's pro-kids list *did* make me feel happy.

On Christmas morning, Jason and I opened the presents we'd gotten for one another and I remember feeling kind of sad, like something was missing. *Is this how it's going to be forever? Just the two of us?* I wondered. It felt like a child should be in the room with us.

Shortly after that, I went to a dinner party at Patricia Altschul's house. Patricia was the matriarch of our show and Whitney's mom. She is the total embodiment of a Southern grande dame and I love her dearly. She'd hired a psychic for the night and we were all supposed to ask her questions about one another.

"Will Cameran have children?" someone asked. Guess I wasn't the only one whose mind was on my uterus.

"Yes," the psychic responded. "By the end of 2017." (She actually said I would have three children, but even today it would take a big change of heart for me to let two more children come through this vagina.) I couldn't breathe when she told me her vision for my future, and I couldn't stop thinking about it afterward. *What if I'm putting off what is supposed to be my greatest job or my greatest purpose? What am I doing?* I wondered.

About a week or two after that dinner, I got home from work and saw that Jason was sitting out at the end of the dock behind our house. The sun was setting, and I walked outside and sat beside him. He seemed very deep in thought and maybe even a little bit upset.

"What's going on? What's wrong?" I asked.

"I was just thinking how nice it would be if I had a child who I could come out here with and teach how to fish," he said. My heart broke into a million pieces. Jason would be the best dad anybody could possibly have, and here I was robbing a child of that opportunity. He is patient, smart and caring. If our child turned out like him, how lucky would I be?

I made another appointment with the therapist.

"A lot of this comes from childhood stuff," she explained. "I'm not blaming your parents, but I suspect there was a time in your life where you didn't have control and you carried that into adulthood. In that case, your indecision is not necessarily a desire *not* to have a child, it's fear."

She was right. I have suffered with fear my whole life and it's a son of a bitch. I've also dealt with anxiety, and both can rob you of your best life. I realized then and there that I didn't want to be controlled by those emotions anymore. Another reality hit me: If I truly didn't want to have kids, I wouldn't have been sitting in that therapist's office. I wouldn't be thinking about this over and over and *over* again. *Maybe this won't be so awful*, I thought. Slowly, my perception shifted and I threw away my birth control.

One day when my mom came over, I shared this with her. I think I told her because I knew how badly she wanted a grandchild, and there would be no turning back once the cat was out of the bag.

"Thinking about it makes me nauseous," I said.

"Maybe it's just *babies* that you're scared of," she said. OMG. Yes! Yes! Yes! Another lightbulb moment.

"You're right! I'm not a baby person. I'm more of a little kid person," I said.

"Cam, before I had you and your sister, I didn't like babies, either," my mom said. Wow.

When I resolved to talk about my baby indecision on national television on *Southern Charm*, I made a conscious choice to be authentic and honest and express my true feelings. People in the South don't discuss this kind of stuff, but I wanted to help other women because I knew I couldn't be the only one struggling with this issue. A lot of viewers said things like, "You shouldn't be having this baby for your husband," and I agree. That *is* a dumb reason to bring a child into this world. But it wasn't just for Jason. In fact, despite really wanting a child, he never pushed me or made me feel like his clock was ticking. Imagining our lives passing us by without a child felt selfish to me. I also came to the realization that I was probably never going to regret HAVING a child (how can you regret something you love unconditionally?), but I might regret NOT having one.

Despite getting some hate from viewers about my indecision, the positive response was much, much more overwhelming. A lot of women DM'd me and said, "I feel the same way, but I felt bad talking about it" or "You have every right to put this amount of thought into your decision." This validation meant the world. And ever since I had Palmer in November of 2017 (can you believe the psychic was right about the timing?), I've been getting at least five messages a day from women saying things like, "I'm in the same boat you were when you were thinking about having a baby. Are you happy with your decision?" Yes, I'm happy. Thrilled, actually.

But buyer beware: despite what social media may suggest, it ain't all roses. Not by a long shot.

I learned that becoming a mom doesn't have to totally rock your world. You choose how you react to change, so ultimately I found myself excited about the next chapter in my life and looking forward to the opportunity to be less selfish. People message me all the time on Instagram and say, "Be honest. Do you ever regret having Palmer?" or "My husband really wants a baby but I'm not sure I do. What do you think I should do?" Do I sometimes look at my friends who don't have children and get a little jealous because they're going out on a Saturday night? Absolutely! Do I scroll past their vacay pics and wish that I were the one sipping a glass of rosé in front of the Eiffel Tower in Paris? Yes! I'm not going to lie about that. But I think that once you have a kid, and once you love that child for the first time, you're never going to regret having them, because at that point you can't imagine your life without them. (That said, if you're serious about going on vacation four times a year and enjoy peeing by yourself, don't have a kid.)

All in all, having a child is surely one of life's greatest experiences, and the best thing I've ever done is be a mama to my little angel. I can't imagine my life without Palmer or without getting to see Jason as a father. I now understand the sorcery that makes women want another baby. (Well, kinda . . . but more on that later.) Still, something as life-changing as having a kid is a really personal decision, and we have to bust the myth that women need to procreate to be fulfilled or happy. I think there's a lot to be said for those who choose not to have children. Heck, they probably live longer and have a lot more money, a lot less stress and better relationships with their significant others. I can only tell you my experience, and that doesn't mean it will be yours. You can talk to those nearest and dearest to you, but take their advice with a grain of salt because only you know what's best for you.

Chapter Four

WHAT BEING PREGGERS IS REALLY LIKE

The amazing thing about becoming a parent is that
you will never again be your own first priority.
—OLIVIA WILDE, MOTHER OF TWO

O nce I decided to go for it, I got knocked up really, *really*
quickly. So quickly, y'all, that some of the first words out
of Jason's mouth when I told him were, "Have you been cheating
on me?" I guess my body had been waiting all along for my mind
to catch up.

Here's what happened. Everyone told me it would take my
system months and months to rid itself of birth control and, as
a result, months and months to get pregnant. So when my pill
prescription ran out, I thought, *I'm thirty-three and Jason is forty-
one and we have been married for three years. I'm not totally sold on
a baby, but since it will take several months to get the process started,*

maybe I just won't refill it. Also, my very best friend, Lynn, had just found out she was pregnant, so if I did get knocked up soon, at least I'd be cooking my kid along with my best friend. Fun, right?

(Just a side note: once I started to take the idea of having a baby very seriously, I decided to have full genetic testing done before getting pregnant. My mother's brother died of cystic fibrosis when he was two years old, so I wanted to be informed if I carried any genes for genetic disease. Luckily, I was fine. There was nothing genetically wrong to make me question the decision to become a mom.)

Well, let me tell you that it's a complete MYTH that it takes lots of time for your body to regulate after being on the pill. I had been on birth control since I was eighteen years old—that's fifteen years—and I got pregnant the month I stopped it. Yes, the same month! My first period after stopping birth control was due in two weeks and, even though it seemed totally crazy and against the odds, for some reason I just knew that I was pregnant. So I googled, "How soon can you test for pregnancy?" and found out that some drugstore tests will show results as early as two weeks before you miss your period. *This is crazy*, I thought as I searched for my car keys. *I literally* just *became* sorta *okay with the idea of having a child. Am I seriously driving to the pharmacy to buy pregnancy tests?* But my trusty inner voice was persistent. "You are pregnant," it told me. "Go get the tests." Oh, let me add that at this point I had told Jason none of this. I obviously knew he wanted a baby, but he would have thought I was crazy to be so sure of myself so soon.

I returned home with three different kinds of pregnancy tests. I was testing so early that I wanted options and felt like more than one test might be needed to confirm my hunch. Even though Jason was back from work at that point, I kept what I was doing under wraps. I yelled "Hi" to him and then went straight upstairs to the bathroom. The first test I peed on was the traditional one with the lines. One line means you're not pregnant; two lines means you are. After waiting two minutes, one line appeared. Not pregnant. It didn't matter, because my intuition was still raging. "You ARE pregnant," it was saying. So I moved on to the next test, a digital option. Instead of lines, this one actually says "Pregnant" or "Not pregnant." (Genius idea!) I peed on the stick and then went to put a load of laundry in the dryer while I waited. When I came back to the bathroom and picked up the test, there was no question about the result. In bold black letters, it read very clearly, "Pregnant." I sat there shocked, but not shocked, if that makes any sense to you. I knew I was pregnant, but I hadn't even missed my period yet. *This is crazy*, I thought. (What's funny is that I bought *that* test from the dollar store—several of my friends swore by these—and it said I was pregnant when the one that cost more than twenty bucks at the drugstore said I wasn't! I'm a bargain hunter anyway, so it's just more proof that expensive doesn't mean better. You're welcome.)

I decided to take the third test before I told Jason. You know, just to REALLY confirm. Again, the result was clear as day: pregnant.

Holy shit, I thought. Jason was downstairs casually watching a football game with no idea how his life was about to change.

He's not going to believe me, I thought. I tried to think of fun ways to tell him. I'm not sure if it's a Southern thing, but 90 percent of my friends have come up with cute, cheeky ways to tell their husbands they are with child: scavenger hunts, giving them a onesie with their favorite sports team embroidered on it, tying the pregnancy test on the damn dog's collar and putting literal buns in their ovens for him to open and see. One girl I know even had a custom fortune cookie made . . . I could go on and on. But I can't keep a secret for more than thirty seconds and my mind was racing, so there was no way in hell I had time to be creative. I just needed to tell somebody this news and Jason was right downstairs. *It won't be cute or original, but just go and do it*, I thought. I walked into Jason's man cave, holding my collection of pee-soaked pregnancy tests.

"Guess what?" I said, waving the tests in the air. "I'm pregnant."

"No you aren't," he said, barely looking in my direction and instead craning his neck around me to catch an instant replay. "You *just* got off birth control."

"I took three tests," I told him, handing him one. He looked at me, but it was clear that this life-changing news had not registered.

"Come on," he said. "This is one of those prank tests you can order online." Now, don't think Jason is insensitive or a jerk, y'all, because that part was my fault. Over the years, I had pranked Jason about some really stupid stuff. One time I told him I'd dropped my engagement ring down the drain, which was believable because I normally clean my rings in the sink. I can totally keep a straight face when pranking someone. That's a skill of mine. He looked at me and said, "Well, it's the only ring you are getting and that's what you get for being careless." Of course, a minute later his practical side came over him and he said, "Don't run the water. I can unhook the pipes and try to find it." Bless his heart! Another time I put a dead lizard on his pillow, and I even bought fake poop and put it on the floor by our toilet. When we were engaged, I told him I was part of the 1 percent of women who get pregnant while on birth control and that I would be sporting a big old belly at the wedding.

"OMG. This is NOT A PRANK! I swear to you I'm pregnant." He then took the cap off one test, and that's when the lightbulb went off (or maybe some pee got on his hand).

"Holy shit! What? How?" he said.

"I don't know," I said, laughing. "But we are having a baby!" We hugged, and then just like that, with three pee-soaked pregnancy tests in hand, our journey to parenthood started.

From the moment I found out I was pregnant, I KNEW I was having a girl. I honestly didn't desire one sex over the other. All I cared about was that the baby was healthy. If anything, I might have wanted a boy slightly more, only because I knew I was probably only going to have one child and figured Jason might naturally want a son. (A lot of men do.) But the moment I found out I was pregnant, I instantly envisioned a little girl. I would have dreams about her, and I know it sounds crazy, but Palmer ended up looking just like the little girl who came to me in my dreams. At ten weeks pregnant, I opted to do the blood test to find out the gender. A few people tried to convince me to wait until the baby was born. "There are so few surprises in life," they said. That may be true, but for me, finding out what I was having ASAP was a given since I naturally have zero patience. I also had to confirm that I was having a girl so I could start throwing my money away on clothes immediately. (This kid wasn't even born and soon she would have a wardrobe bigger than my own! Dressing a little girl is so much fun.) A week after I did the test, I called the lab for the verdict.

"We can mail you the results so it can be a surprise for you and your husband," the nurse told me.

"No thanks. Just tell me now," I said.

"You want me to tell you over the *phone*?" she asked.

"Yes," I said. What part of "just tell me now" did this lady not understand?

"You don't want to wait for your husband?"

"No, no. Just tell me."

"It's a girl!" the nurse exclaimed. I knew it!

When Jason got home from work a couple of hours later, I told him that my suspicions had been correct. Jason is one of three boys, so a girl would be a new experience for him, but one he was super excited about. So no gender reveal party, no fancy cake that's colored inside or popping balloons to reveal blue or pink confetti. Do I regret finding out alone and over the phone? Well, um . . . kinda. Why can't I ever be patient?

Because I've always had a very fast metabolism, I have a hard time putting on weight. (I know, I know, cue the violins. But actually, for the most part being so thin actually made me very insecure for a long time. In middle school, I looked like I had an eating disorder and was teased horribly.) So I loved having curves for the first time in my life, as well as boobs, when I was pregnant. Yes, boobs. Actually I had melons! For someone who had stuffed her bra since puberty, this was amazing. If you're like me, you'll find this very exciting, but just know that nothing lasts forever, and even those perky cantaloupes turn into tea bags when you stop breastfeeding. (Sorry!) I hoped at first that I would easily find non-maternity clothes that would transition my changing body through pregnancy. To me, maternity wear signaled frumpiness, so I tried to avoid it for as long as I could. At first, I would wear my pre-pregnancy jeans and just leave them unzipped and unbuttoned. (Think: your great-uncle after Thanksgiving dinner. Not a great look.) After this, I tried buying larger sizes in everything. Well, this lasted until I was twenty-seven weeks along and woke up one day and thought, *Screw this . . . I'm uncomfortable.* I went to a maternity store and tried on the most glorious pair of maternity pants. I could actually breathe! I bought three pairs and had to take back every single negative thing I had said about maternity wear. It became my BFF! I had no idea how cute and affordable some of it would be. It got very real when I googled maternity underwear. Of course, by the end you could have put me in a muumuu with cats on it—and I felt like I needed a muumuu—and I wouldn't have cared. Jason wasn't going anywhere at that point, and who was I trying to impress?

While we're on the subject of clothes, I am so embarrassed by the amount of clothes/shoes/accessories I bought for Palmer prior to her birth. Here's a tip for new moms: babies don't need shoes. Especially newborns. In fact, newborns look absolutely ridiculous in a pair of shoes. Save your money! Spend it on a nice bottle of wine. Another waste of money: the *copious* amount of hair bows that I bought. You are not a proper Southern baby girl without a giant bow on top of your head, and Southern women will find a way to affix one to even the slightest sprig of hair. Even one strand of hair gets a big, fat bow. Well, Miss Palmer Wimberly was a rebel from the start and decided bows were not for her. She immediately yanked out every single one I tried to put in her hair. Come to think of it, her first phrase at one year old was actually "No bow!" To this day she still won't wear one. I gave away every single one I bought—and there were probably seventy-five of them.

I'm not going to lie: before I got pregnant, I was not one of those women who thought pregnancy was beautiful. In fact, I was the opposite; I thought it was kinda gross—a point of view I never shared with anyone. I was also petrified to cook a kid for nine months. I thought I would hate it and feel like I had an alien inside of me. On top of this, as a control freak, I find the unknown terrifying. Up until I got pregnant, I had control over pretty much all aspects of my life, including my body. But I ended up being amazed and in awe of the whole experience. Seeing my body change was pretty cool. It gave me a newfound respect for being a woman and seeing what we are actually capable of. *Holy shit, I am literally growing a tiny human in my gut.* I was so grateful that my body was able to carry out this process, especially knowing that so many women have difficulty doing so. Even if you're petrified of being preggo like I was, just remember that something like 90 percent of the things you worry about will never happen anyway. (It's a quote I think I heard once.) Well, it's true. Pregnancy was WAY easier than I thought it would be and if you just try to relax and take it all in, the reward at the end is worth every minute of morning sickness, the gas and the stretch marks, too.

Chapter Five

WHAT I DIDN'T EXPECT
WHEN I WAS EXPECTING

If you are a mom, you are a superhero. Period.

—ROSIE POPE, MOTHER OF FOUR

Although there were lots of things about being knocked up that I anticipated, there were plenty I did not. Stuff no one told me about. I didn't know that Gas-X and MiraLAX would become my ol' faithfuls for nine months (MiraLAX was my nightcap many evenings) and that instead of feeling cute and sassy, I'd feel bloated and constipated. My once firm butt deflated and looked like a block of cottage cheese and my belly was no longer hard. My back also started to hurt as I got bigger. (Support wear was a game changer because it lifted my bump and supported my core.) Clearly, it's God's intelligent design that women, not men, are built to carry children. I don't think they could handle it. I also became a germaphobe during the last few months. Jason works in a hospital, and I was not having any of those germs in my house. So I would make him strip off his scrubs and get naked in the garage every day before he came inside. He told me I was psycho, but this turned out to be good practice for the coronavirus pandemic just a few years later. To my surprise, it also never bothered me that strangers touched my stomach. I found it endearing in a weird way . . . well, except the one time a man touched it. That was odd and kinda creepy. Note to men: don't touch a pregnant woman's stomach unless you are related to her and have permission.

I also didn't expect that seemingly everyone would offer their unsolicited opinions on pregnancy and child-rearing. I'd get questions and comments from friends, strangers, the cashier at Wendy's, you name it. They'd ask, "Are you gonna get an epidural?" "Are you gonna wash all her clothes before she wears them for the first time?" "Are you gonna put her in the crib on the first night?" My answer was always the same: "I have no idea what the hell I'm gonna do. I've never done this before!" To be honest, I didn't even know those things were, well, a thing.

Then there were the hundreds of messages on Instagram asking if I planned on breastfeeding my child. So many of them that I actually thought about deleting my account forever. Why did so many strangers care if I was going to put my child on the boob or not? My response? First, it was none of anyone's dang business how I planned to feed my child. I was going to *try* to breastfeed, but if it didn't work, I was not stressing out. I planned to pump. If pumping didn't work, I was happily going to stick a bottle of formula in my baby's mouth and she'd turn out just fine. That's the way I was fed, along with millions and millions of other people, and we're all okay. Now, if good old formula didn't work, my final plan was to go to Chick-fil-A, get a number-three value size, put that in a blender and spoon-feed her, something I was fairly certain she'd like because she'd just eaten a heck of a lot of it for nine months anyway. And when it was time for her to eat baby food, hell no, I was not going to be making my own as so many inquiring minds wanted to know. Instead of pureeing my own peas, I'd be buying Gerber in a jar. Hopefully buy one, get one free.

Speaking of eating, I was always hungry. Food was like a drug to me when I was pregnant. And when you're cooking a kid, everything tastes so, SO much better. I read an article that the foods you feed your growing fetus will later turn out to be those that he/she likes as a child. That could be a problem, because I did not nourish my womb with the fruits of Mother Earth. Nope. I didn't diet one day I was pregnant and allowed myself to eat whatever I wanted. Besides the aforementioned Chick-fil-A, I ate a lot of Wendy's, Ben & Jerry's ice cream and gas station food like doughnuts and Vienna sausages. (Don't judge. They're so good. The juice!) I also craved Philly cheesesteaks big-time, and there was about a two-month period when I probably ate at least one a day. The local cheesesteak shop opened at 11 A.M. and I would be there in the parking lot at 10:50 A.M. waiting for it to open. And I felt no shame. Heck, I grew up eating Happy Meals. That's what nourished us as kids. I'm just sayin'! I still had my cup of coffee in the A.M., but I did limit my caffeine intake to only one drink a day and I took my prenatal vitamin religiously every morning. Oh, another thing . . . I can't believe I'm admitting this, but I did not stomach one single piece of fruit my entire pregnancy. Not an apple, an orange or even a single grape. Why? Pregnant or not pregnant, I literally never eat fruit. EVER. I have taken bites and they have all been spit out. I can't swallow it. My body is not capable. No lie: if you told me you would pay me a million dollars to eat a banana or an orange, I couldn't do it. It's a texture thing. It's funny, too, because when I got my blood work back early in the pregnancy the nurse looked at me and said, "You must be a healthy eater." I laughed. Boy, did I have her fooled. And not just that nurse. I actually lied to my ob-gyn and told her I *did* eat fruit (sorry, doctor!), but I didn't. (I did eat a few veggies during pregnancy, but my diet primarily consisted of meat and carbs, and that's probably why I developed cellulite on every square inch of my body.) But don't judge me, because Palmer is fine and smart and over 50 percent on the growth charts. So I actually think the cheesesteaks helped. In the end, I gained about thirty-five pounds, which is within the recommended range. I have always been naturally thin, so I think my body needed the extra weight for a healthy pregnancy.

As the months progressed, I felt the baby toss and turn all the time—and it's pretty freaky to see your stomach move and know it's not gas. It amazed me so much that I found myself reaching for my cellphone to record the movements to show people later. The first time I felt Palmer kick, it was surreal. It actually felt more like a little flutter. *Wow . . . there is actually a tiny human inside of me!* I thought. Feeling Palmer move definitely made pregnancy feel

REAL. It's funny, because before I got pregnant I was actually kind of repulsed by the concept of feeling a tiny body move inside my stomach. *How do women actually enjoy this?* I wondered. I surprised myself because not only did I enjoy the kicks and movements, I actually found it to be fascinating and cool. It was also very comforting as a sign that she was growing and healthy, so I looked forward to her daily little backflips and somersaults. Toward the end of my pregnancy, her movements looked like a scene from *Alien*, and Jason and I would just watch in absolute wonder!

Overall, I had an extremely easy pregnancy. I had no severe medical complications, I had relatively good energy and I only felt nauseated the first few weeks, but even that was never bad. In fact, the worst part of being pregnant was constantly having to pee during my third trimester. I'm not sure if Palmer was sitting on my bladder in a weird way, but I literally had to pee All. The. Time. Part of my nightly ritual is to take a bath. Once when I was around thirty-nine weeks, I was lying in the tub, feeling totally relaxed. The bath had finally filled up and I had to pee so bad, but I didn't want to expend the energy it would take to get up out of the water and dry off just to use the toilet. So I just lay there and peed in the tub. I remembered Jason saying one time that pee was sterile, so I thought, *What the heck.* That was a low point!

All in all, I was pleasantly surprised that all the fears I had pre-pregnancy were gone and if anything, my anxiety actually decreased. Instead, I felt a sense of calm—yes, total calm—for most of those nine months. In fact, I was *so* mellow that I kept waiting for my hormones to kick in. Many women told me they were emotional messes when they were pregnant, but I didn't feel that way at all. No highs and lows. No crying fits. In fact, I never shed a tear. Not one. (Which left me wondering if I had a dead heart.) I think it was because I still couldn't even process that this was MY child.

I guess I wasn't your typical mom-to-be. I was clueless and in denial, and that was fine with me. In addition to my drive-thru diet, I was not ready to give up my explicit rap music. Come on, can babies really hear from inside the womb? And if so, isn't Notorious B.I.G.'s "Get Money" just a lesson in economics? And by the time I was nearing my due date, I still hadn't taken any Lamaze classes or read the pregnancy bible *What to Expect When You're Expecting*. Early on, I was scared off when I signed up for a pregnancy newsletter and the first email was headed "Nine facts about your vagina." Oh Lord! The only thing I'd done was watch a YouTube video of childbirth, which made me dry-heave. (Don't try that at home!) But as the weeks and months progressed, I decided to do my due diligence and meet with a birthing instructor. It was really nice, and having her actually come into our home and do it in private was comforting. She gave me a huge binder of information that I still have.

"If you could visualize your perfect birthing experience, what would that be?" she asked.

"I would pick my baby off a tree and not have to have her emerge from my body," I said. Not an emotional answer, but the God's honest truth. I didn't want to go through labor, have my vag all messed up and swollen, and then wind up with the baby coming out the sunroof—a.k.a. a C-section. Around thirty-seven weeks, my ob-gyn asked me if I had a birth plan. I shook my head.

"Do whatever is best for me and the baby," I told her.

"Smart . . . thank you," she said. I could tell she probably didn't get this response that often. As an anesthesiologist, Jason witnesses babies being born every single day. I knew from his many stories of birth plans gone wrong that the smartest thing I could do was not have one at all and leave my fate in the hands of the medical professionals who do this daily. For the second time in my life since deciding to get pregnant, I gave up control.

However, I did do one important thing to keep myself calm and this is where I want to talk about visualization, because I think it's important and that it actually works. In my early twenties, I read a book called *Manifest Your Destiny* by Dr. Wayne Dyer and it was life-changing for me. In a nutshell, Dr. Dyer teaches that you ultimately become what you think about, which is why our thoughts are super important. When I was pregnant, every night before I went to sleep I purposely envisioned an easy, uncomplicated vaginal birth. I would close my eyes and see myself lying on the hospital bed in the delivery room with my feet being held. I visualized myself breathing and pushing and the baby coming out easily. It was never a wish, it was never a prayer . . . it was just a knowing. Of course, I was always okay with the idea of a C-section if that's what was best for me and the baby, but in all honesty I wanted to prove wrong that nosey ob-gyn friend of Jason's who I told you about earlier. It was years before I even thought of getting pregnant, when she had looked at my hips and told me I was a "textbook C-section." Also let me add, having a C-section is in no way a failure. Sometimes it's a necessity, and some women might even prefer to opt to do it. Again, YOU need to do YOU! All that matters is that mama and baby are healthy.

Although I have never been a neat freak and small amounts of clutter don't bother me, that all changed around week thirty-eight of my pregnancy. I had read about the nesting instinct and found it fascinating. Nesting is basically insane housekeeping during the last weeks of pregnancy in preparation for the baby to arrive. Well, it's like some other being overtook my body. All of a sudden, I was organizing everything and I was also throwing out everything. I found myself yelling at Jason, "Do we really need this? We haven't used this in three years. It's going in the trash" or "This could hurt the baby" or "This could poison the baby." I threw out bags and bags of stuff. I also cleaned the house thoroughly for probably the first time ever. We have never had a cleaning service because . . . well, I'm cheap, so I have always been the maid. But I had been a crappy one. OMG, suddenly I was like, "There is dust on the blinds," and had to clean them. I took books off the shelves and wiped behind them . . . something that had never been done. I mopped. I disinfected. I turned into a Merry Maid on crack for about a two-week period. My house had never been so sparkling clean.

As you can see, I was blessed to have a generally easy, uncomplicated pregnancy and seemed to be handling it pretty well. That was until week thirty-nine. By then I was over it. And I mean OVER IT. I was still whiling away the days in pregnancy purgatory. I couldn't sleep, was super uncomfortable and just wanted to hold my baby—in my arms, not my stomach! Filming *Southern Charm* so late in my pregnancy was difficult, too. I was tired, on edge and really had no desire to party or be out late like the rest of the cast. Luckily, my friends and the production crew knew and totally understood, and they did everything in their power to accommodate me.

After an appointment approaching my thirty-ninth week, I learned I could be voluntarily induced a week early to term, which is forty weeks. This is where you go in and are started on a Pitocin drip to jump-start labor. I was impatient, and this appealed to me as a relatively controlled situation.

"How soon can I be induced?" I asked my ob-gyn.

"On Tuesday," she said.

"Great! Pencil me in," I replied happily. Make that VERY happily. When I called Jason on the way home from the appointment to tell him, he was very laid-back.

"Is it scary to get induced?" I asked him.

"No. It happens every day," he said. Before you think he's heartless, Jason *is* an anesthesiologist who gives epidurals to pregnant women all day long, so he was understandably desensitized. But this was the first time for his wife! A little sympathy would have been nice. Still, I was excited about being induced. I thought, *This is awesome!* No water breaking in the grocery store. No rushing to pack my hospital bag. I would simply check into my hospital room, get hooked up to some IV drugs to start my labor and have a baby in twenty-four hours! Ha ha ha.

The following week, nothing had changed in my nether regions, so I packed my bags and headed to the hospital to get induced. I remember leaving my house, wistfully thinking, *Wow. This is the last time I will be at my house without a kid.* Boy, was I wrong. My baby was saying, "Not so fast, Mom," because here's what happened. At the hospital, I was put on the Pitocin drip, which makes your body have contractions that you can track on a monitor. Although my contractions were so massive that they looked like earthquake activity and I could feel them, my vag was not having it. For whatever reason, inductions don't work on this body, and my cervix was not responding to the Pitocin! By hour twenty-three, the nurse had turned the Pitocin up to the legal limit the hospital would allow. When nothing happened, she told me, "Your cervix is a steel trap."

Clearly, my baby was running the show and she was NOT ready. The ob-gyn on call told me the next step was to break my water in hopes that would jump-start labor. When she left the room, Jason turned to me and said, "We aren't doing that."

"What do you mean 'we aren't doing that'? What do we do, then?" I asked him, practically in tears.

"We are going home," he said.

I looked at him wide-eyed. "What? Go home? Without a baby? Huh?"

"Yes," Jason calmly said. "The smartest thing to do is go home and let your body go into labor naturally. If they break your water and the baby isn't ready, you increase your chances of an emergency C-section." I wasn't aware of this at the time, but once your water breaks in full-term labor you have about twenty-four hours to get the baby out.

"Am I allowed to go home?" I asked the nurse when she came back into the room.

"Absolutely," she said, before adding, "that's what I would do." Of course I trusted Jason's point of view and the nurse's, but boy oh boy was I disappointed.

"Your baby will come when she's ready," my doctor told me as she signed my hospital discharge papers. "You'll just have to wait." Easy for *her* to say. I'd been pregnant for what seemed like forever. I was over it and on my last nerve. I was more than ready to have this kid living on the outside, but it was out of my hands. Even from the womb, this baby was not doing things according to MY grand plan. It was all her own, which is pretty much the essence of parenting, so maybe God was trying to tell me something.

After the nurse unhooked my IVs, I packed up my bag and left the room. In the elevator, I encountered a woman holding her newborn in a car seat, which made me feel awful. I was doing a walk of shame out of the hospital WITHOUT a baby. Twenty-four hours earlier, I never would have imagined leaving the hospital holding only my pillow.

So we went home . . . and I bitched and moaned for another week and a half. During that time, I was pretty much housebound and eating everything in sight. (This included a giant barrel of cheddar cheese balls I found at Target. I've had a long-standing love affair with these fluorescent orange, Styrofoam-like snacks ever since I was a child, when I used to take my allowance money to the grocery store and buy them.) Well, eating and sitting around just made me feel large and NOT in charge. In case you have not had a baby and you're wondering, it feels like you're constantly bloated and constipated with a big poop that you just can't get out. (Sorry if that's TMI.) Of course, that poop is actually a baby. I was also bored, because there was not a lot that I could do. My biggest excitement was forcing myself to take a shower every day so I felt somewhat human. To say I was going a bit stir-crazy is an understatement. It didn't help that all my friends were going to Hilton Head for the weekend. So while they were working on their tans at the beach and getting wasted, I was home googling "vaginal tears." Boy, how quickly life can change!

Now I was forty weeks pregnant, and did I mention that I was OVER IT? Hoping to light a fire under this baby's butt, I tried every old wives' tale in the book to get labor going. I'm glad that standing on your head and chanting the Lord's Prayer while drinking spoiled goat's milk worked for women of yore, but it didn't work for me. I did jumping jacks, I ate chicken parmesan and spicy food and I bounced on my birthing ball. Nothing. Nada. No action. I even did a lap down Labor Lane with my friend and castmate Shep Rose driving. Labor Lane is actually Chalmers Street, a bumpy cobblestone road in downtown Charleston. It's old Southern lore that pregnant women back in the 1800s would ride down this bumpy street to induce labor. I thought a couple of laps would dilate my cervix, but all that happened was I peed. For real. At first Shep just laughed, but then he kind of freaked out because he didn't want pee on his car seat. Thankfully it wasn't that much, but it was enough that when we went to lunch afterward, I went in the bathroom and threw my underwear in the trash can. Oh the joys and beauty of pregnancy.

It's funny that before I was preggers, I worried that I couldn't properly carry a baby to term. Was I wrong, wrong, wrong! I carried Palmer over my due date to forty-one weeks. My bun in the oven was cooked and she was well done. The bottom line when it comes to pregnancy: there is no such thing as normal, so be prepared to be surprised. And hungry. Very, very hungry.

Chapter Six

LABOR DAY

❦

*The moment a child is born, the mother is also
born. She never existed before.
The woman existed, but the mother, never.
A mother is something absolutely new.*
—BHAGWAN SHREE RAJNEESH

I think one of the reasons I debated getting pregnant for so long was the dreaded delivery day. No joke, y'all. I was so worried that I was going to have a nervous breakdown when I went into labor. I know, I know—women have been giving birth since the beginning of time and almost four million women a year have babies in the U.S. But when it's *your* first time and *your* body that's got to do the work, statistics just don't matter. I was terribly worried that my experience would be like that of several friends who pushed and pushed for hours but then ended up having to have a C-section. What to do? When I was pregnant and I would worry or get anxious about birthing a child, I would tell myself over and over, *Cam, get a grip. Cavewomen did this and if they could do it, you can, too, so calm the f*** down.* Someone said this to me early on in my pregnancy (I wish I could remember who it was and thank that person profusely) and, man, did it stick with me. I mean, come on. If a woman who lived in a cave—a frickin' *cave*—could successfully give birth, what the hell was I worrying about? All they had to rely on was instinct, while I was going to have a team of nurses and doctors at my disposal and a bed that reclined. I was going to have a soft pillow and medicine that would numb any pain . . . and ice chips and apple juice. This really put things in perspective. So every time I got riddled with anxiety, I imagined a pregnant cavewoman hobbling around her cave and instantly felt better.

Well, what do you know . . . just like pregnancy was totally different than I expected, so was labor and delivery. (Lesson learned: worrying can be a real waste of time and usually just stresses you out even more.) By the time delivery day rolled around, my anxiety had pretty much dissipated and I was uncharacteristically focused. So here's what happened.

At my forty-week appointment, my ob-gyn responded to my frustration by saying, "Start walking. Walk, walk, walk . . . and when you feel like you can't walk anymore . . . keep walking."

So at forty-one weeks on the dot, I looked at Jason and said, "Today, we walk." We drove to my mom's house, which was only five minutes from the hospital where I would deliver. At about 1 P.M., we started walking . . . and walking . . . and walking. We walked several neighborhoods. Then my mom joined us. After about four hours, she and Jason were tired, but not me. So we kept walking. Once we got back to my mom's house around 5:00 that evening, I started feeling crampy. Nothing unbearable. *OMG . . . are these contractions?* I wondered. We started timing them, and they were indeed. I decided I was going to try to tolerate them as long as possible before going to the hospital. Since I had already been in that hospital bed for my false alarm, I knew I didn't want to be in it any longer than I needed to be. A couple of hours later the contractions got pretty intense, so I got into my mom's tub to try to get some relief.

"Maybe we should head to the hospital, Cam," Jason said. I could tell he was getting a little antsy.

"Nope . . . let me see if I can take it a little longer," I said. At that point my teeth started chattering.

"Cameran, get in the car. It's time."

The ride to the hospital was not like what you see in the movies. I wasn't screaming. I wasn't crying. I stayed very calm, but I *was* holding on to the door handle and trying just to breathe.

We arrived at the hospital, I got checked into my room and the first thing I said to the nurse was, "Give me the epidural." And I meant it. Let me tell you, I bow to the women who do this all natural. But unless you want to scream like a dying horse, my advice is to get the epidural. Once my epidural was in, around 8 P.M., I was in heaven. Then I was in labor for about twelve hours waiting for my cervix to dilate ten centimeters, which is what tells your ob-gyn that it's go-time and your baby can fit through your vag. Side note: Do you know what ten centimeters is? I had no clue until I saw a "Cervical Dilation" chart using well-known items for comparison. One centimeter is a blueberry, four centimeters is a lime, seven centimeters is an apple and ten is a cantaloupe. Yes, a frickin' cantaloupe-sized hole in your cervix! And *that* is why mamas need all those presents on Mother's Day.

Speaking of mamas, my mother-in-law and mother were also in the room to witness me giving birth to their new grandchild, sitting next to each other on the right side of my bed. It wasn't planned that way. They had both come to the hospital when I went into labor the night before and had been in the waiting room for hours and hours and hours. Around 6 A.M., they came into the delivery room to see me and just never left. It was my mom's first grandchild and my mother-in-law's seventh, although it was the first one that she actually got to see being born. I think it was a really cool experience for both of them.

Anyway, after I was finally dilated, I started pushing and pushing. For Jason this was basically just another day in the office. As an anesthesiologist, he's the one pregnant women scream for in pain and also the one they want to hug afterward. Several women have actually offered to name their children after him once he's placed the epidural and they've felt immediate relief. So when I was in labor, he understood way more about giving birth than I did. Jason's personality is also cool and collected to begin with, so when I was laboring, he was calm as could be. He was just sitting and observing the whole thing, and maybe even a bit numb. The nurse finally encouraged him to be a part of it and hold my leg.

"Sir, maybe you want to get up and help your wife," she said. It's almost like as a doctor he forgot that this time it was different, it was HIS wife and HIS baby being born. But that snapped him out of it. He sprang into action and held my leg.

I pushed for about an hour before my little peanut popped out. It was relatively fast, but here's *another* thing that no one told me. Friends talked about the joy of getting their epidural and how, after just a few pushes, their babies were out. Not me. During the last twenty minutes, I actually started hyperventilating from pushing so hard and, as a result, this increased my heart rate to the point that the alarms were going off on the monitor. This is called tachycardia, when your heart rate is way, way above normal. My blood pressure started dropping as well, which made me feel like I was going to pass out. For a split second, I thought, *Well, this is it. I'm about to be rolled back for an emergency C-section.*

"What do you think we should do?" the ob-gyn asked Jason.

"She needs to slow her breathing and take a break," Jason replied. So they gave me a paper bag and told me to breathe into it. Jason came to my side and started massaging the carotid artery in my neck to slow my heart rate. I had no idea why he was doing this at the time and didn't even ask; I figured he knew what he was doing. LOL. After about three to four minutes, everything calmed down and I was able to push again.

The truth is that I actually didn't want Jason to see what was going on, um, down below, because I didn't want him to have that memory of my vagina wide open. But he was the one who cut the cord, so he saw everything. Oh well. Ladies, just get ready to poop yourself in front of your husband . . . everybody does. And if the nurse tells you that you didn't, she's lying. Yes, you typically will poop the bed when you have a baby. (Yes, even you, Jennifer.) Why? Because when you push that hard, any and everything that is in your colon will come out. There is no getting around it. As the old saying goes, "Shit happens." Yup. It sure does. Also, you will be totally oblivious to the fact that you just shit yourself if you have an epidural. I only knew this happened to me because I straight-up asked Jason if it had happened yet. So if you are one of those women who always closes the bathroom door when taking a number two . . . well, you have another thing coming to you. Maybe tell your significant other to wait outside the labor room until the coast is clear.

When I was pregnant, I would watch these YouTube delivery videos that showed little bundles of joy popping out headfirst from their mamas' vaginas with cone heads. Contrary to popular belief, a lot of newborns come out not so cute and then pretty up later. I was totally prepared for Palmer to be funny-looking, so it took me by surprise to look down and see a perfectly round little head. No cone in sight. "Oh my God, look at her head," I said to Jason, feeling a sense of pride. "It's so perfect." Then it hit me. *Oh shit. Something had to give for her head to be that perfect!* I thought. That's when Jason told me about the tear. And I didn't just have a tiny tear. It was a bad one that required several stitches. As I was icing my vagina later that day, I made one definitive decision: *Nothing is coming out of this ever again!* Luckily the vagina is a very resilient organ due to good blood flow and it bounces back pretty quickly . . . so ladies, don't fret if it gets injured. You'll be alright.

When I was pregnant, I told Jason not to be one of those guys who say that "we" are pregnant or "we" are in labor, because "we" are not pregnant and "we" are not in labor. And that was *before* my labor experience, when I didn't really know what I was talking about. *Now* I feel even more strongly about this, and I will tell any guy who says "we" are in labor to check himself, because it's NOT a team thing. The woman is doing the heavy lifting.

Anyway, about twelve hours after getting my epidural, Palmer Corrine Wimberly finally touched down at 8:32 A.M. Although everyone thinks Palmer is a family name, it's not. Jason came up with it when I was around five months pregnant. I honestly have no idea where he got it from. I didn't like it at first. I wanted to name her June or Larkin, but I finally caved and agreed that it was a strong name for a girl. Now I can't imagine her being named anything else. Her middle name, Corrine, is the same as mine, which was my great-grandmother's name. She was seven pounds three ounces and twenty inches long. It was the wildest experience of my life, and so were the days that followed. Labor, delivery and post-pregnancy recovery was a total shock to my body and mind. How you feel when you go into labor and immediately after having a baby is something that I was not prepared for. I finally understood the expression "I feel like I've been hit by a Mack truck."

Before I had Palmer, most of the moms I talked to said they felt a connection the first time they held their babies. But there were no fireworks for me. As soon as the nurse placed Palmer in my arms, I was so drained and exhausted from labor and in shock from how tiring it was for my body that all I wanted to do was sleep. Yup, that sounds really awful, but it's the truth. I kept my eyes open long enough to count her fingers and toes, and then I passed out. I'd never heard anyone say that before. All I'd seen were sweet pictures of mom and baby posing for the camera—or at least mom posing, baby snoozing. I'm not sure if it's a Southern thing, but before I had Palmer, I really wasn't made aware of the negative aspects of having a baby. When I would ask other women what it was like to give birth to their first child, the overwhelming majority would say things to the tune of, "It's the most love you will ever feel," "Your heart will grow ten times" and "You will want to bottle up the feeling of holding your baby for the first time." Yes. All of these things are very true . . . but it can also be a huge shock to your system. When the baby is born, the mother is born, too, and it's a side of yourself you've never met. Honestly, though, I get why women fib a little. We don't want to scare other women, and we don't want to sound weak. But I would have loved a little heads-up about certain things.

So to say that I wasn't prepared for labor to be so exhausting and draining is an understatement. I also wasn't prepared for the hospital. I basically packed my whole house for my room, including an aromatherapy diffuser and a brand-new, cute little monogrammed robe that I thought I'd wear. You name it, I had it. All of it useless, except my toothbrush. (When you've got a tear the size of Texas, a fluffy robe, no matter how cute, is not going to help the situation. A flimsy, open-backed hospital gown is much more practical.) Now, the hospital had all the delightful things I *really* needed: maxi pads, mesh undies, ice packs, Epsom salts, a sitz bath and diapers for me. Yes, *me*. I wish someone had told me that not only would my child be wearing a diaper, but I would be wearing one, too. I remember seeing Kate Middleton coming down the stairs of the hospital after her first baby, Prince George, was born. She was wearing heels and hose, with her hair coiffed to perfection. I thought for sure that was going to be the same way I'd be walking out with my baby. That's a crock of shit. God bless her, but Kate was wearing a diaper for sure. It was probably a royal diaper, not a Depends like I had on, but the Duchess of Cambridge was wearing a diaper.

It's kind of messed up and ass backwards that after being in labor for hours and then giving birth, you have to go through this major recovery at the same time you're caring for a newborn. And if it's your first time, you have no idea what you're doing because you've never experienced it before! I mean, come on. I don't know when things changed, but it used to be that when a woman had a baby in the hospital, they would take her little one to the nursery at night and the nurses would bring the baby to her when the baby needed to breastfeed or have a bottle. This way the mom could rest and get her much, much-needed sleep. Today, it seems like most hospitals—including the one I delivered in—have changed the protocol to what they call "baby friendly." Instead of taking the baby to the nursery during the night, they leave the baby right beside you in the room. Here you have just given birth. Your body is traumatized, you're in shock and healing from either a C-section or vaginal birth, and you're expected to have this baby lying next to you all night when you desperately need to snooze. To me, that's just a mind-blowing setup. However, when I talked to other moms about this baby-friendly situation, the opinions on it were pretty much split. Lots of moms said they would have loved the break of a nursery taking the baby so they could sleep, but others said they would have been freaked out for the baby to leave the room. I totally can see both sides, but I think it would have been nice to have had the option.

After being up for twenty-four hours in active labor and then giving birth, I needed to rest and did not prefer to have my baby in the room with me. (My hospital literally put a tracking device on Palmer's ankle the second she was born, so I was never worried about her getting stolen or misplaced.) A delivery through your vag like I had is enough of a recovery, but a C-section is a whole different story. It's a way longer recovery, more traumatic mentally and physically. So I bow down to women who had to go through that. I cannot imagine it. I can't help but wonder if that feeling of total exhaustion and the expectation of a speedy recovery after the physical shock of labor contributes to high rates of depression and postpartum issues. I tried to find research on this and didn't see much. However, according to the National Sleep Foundation, people who experience postpartum depression don't sleep as well as those without this condition.

Jason was great when I was recovering, but I'll never forget the nurses! Oh man, they deserve a shout-out. It's these people who help put ice packs in your mesh undies, who clean up your poop and drain your pee bladder and talk you off the cliff. They do a job that most can't, and I have so much respect for them. Nurses, GOD BLESS YOU!

Speaking of bladders, here's a really funny story from the hospital. It's also a little heads-up for those of you who are pregnant and get embarrassed easily. The morning after I had Palmer, my mom, her longtime partner of ten years, Mark, and Palmer's godmother, my dear friend Anitha, came to visit me and see the baby. Everyone was oohing and ahhing over Palmer and taking their turns holding her while I was lying in bed, recovering and resting. A nurse came into the room and walked toward Palmer's bassinet.

"Hi, everyone. I'm here to do Palmer's required hearing test," she said. I had no idea this was even a thing, but I guess it makes sense to confirm your child can hear before releasing him or her from the hospital.

"Everyone can stay in the room, but I need complete silence so we can properly administer the test," the nurse added.

"No problem," we all told her. Then she took little P over to the machine to begin the test.

"Okay, quiet, everyone," she reminded us. This sounded simple enough, but then all of a sudden I had to pee. Badly. I couldn't hold it. My catheter had just been removed and I had very little bladder control at this point. Well, turns out I had very little control of something else, too. I tried to make as little noise as possible as I hobbled to the bathroom when it started . . . I farted. Loud.

Then another one and another one . . . and another. The complete silence of the room was totally shattered by a string of loud farts that sounded like a machine gun going off. There was nothing I could do. I just stood there, frozen . . . with both hands over my face, mortified beyond belief. The nurse got tickled and then I started chuckling. Anitha was laughing so hard that she was bent over in tears, and my mom and Mark couldn't contain themselves, either. Needless to say, Palmer's hearing test had to start over again.

Although my labor and childbirth were out-of-body experiences for *me*, the hospital saw them as about as routine as you could get. So thanks to what they called an "uncomplicated vaginal labor," they released me from the hospital after only twenty-four hours. That's ONE DAY! What the heck? Even though I was ready to get out of that hospital bed, it seemed a bit premature. Back when our moms and grandmas gave birth, they often hung out in the hospital for a whole week or more. After all, you are like a wounded bird and have to go through this major recovery, but you're being sent home to care for an infant. All while having no idea what you're doing! How insane. So it was a surreal feeling when my sweet nurse Lizzy rolled me out of the hospital in a wheelchair to our car. *Wait, what? Is this it? There is no instruction manual?* I thought. Nope, there is not. And without an instruction manual, I had my first failure of motherhood. It came when I tried to buckle Palmer into her infant car seat. I couldn't figure out how to work the damn thing with all those straps, belts and buckles. Jason couldn't figure it out either, and we both stood there sweating and practically tearing our hair out. I swear it felt like trying to solve a Rubik's Cube. So I FaceTimed my best friend Lynn, who had her first baby seven weeks before me. I knew she had the same car seat.

"HELP!" I cried. "What the heck do I do with this?" Luckily, Lynn talked me through it and, finally, we were on our way home with our precious cargo. Let the fun begin!

Chapter Seven

THE NEW MOM DAZE & HAZE

There is something so magical about having a baby
in the house. Time expands and contracts;
each moment holds its own little eternity.

—MICHELLE OBAMA, MOTHER OF TWO

To say that life changes when you have a baby—especially your first one—is a major understatement, and for me, the adjustment to new motherhood was the hardest part. As you parents out there know, it's not all puppies and rainbows, and I was rattled. The second night home from the hospital, I was lying in bed at 3 A.M. sobbing uncontrollably to Jason while he held me in his arms. "What have we done? Our life was *so* great," I cried. "Why did we do this? Why did we ruin our life? I just want to sleep." Looking back on this, I can't help but chuckle. Today, I know that was just my hormones talking, but back then I wasn't laughing. I was in a true fog for the first six to eight weeks after Palmer was born.

Physically, it's a shock to your system akin to Navy SEAL training. I did a lot of googling during those first weeks. One search was, "Is it normal to feel like you were hit by a truck after giving birth?" No joke. Not only was my crotch in pain from that pretty traumatic tear in my nether region, but my once exciting life was now diapers and breastfeeding 24/7. Luckily, it was just Palmer's diapers by this point, not mine, too. It was a roller coaster going from total independence and focusing only on me, myself and I to *Holy shit! I have a tiny human who relies on me for EVERYTHING. Her survival depends on me!* That was scary.

A big post-pregnancy surprise was not really being able to walk for the first three days home (thanks to the tear in my perineum). My body felt the weakest it ever had in my life. I would have also loved a little warning about the stuff that emerges from your body during that first week. And there's lots of it. (Sorry to be graphic, but I want to be real here. Somebody's gotta tell you.) Convinced that I was dying, I called my ob-gyn and told her about all the bloody clots coming out of me. "As long as they're smaller than a golf ball, you're okay," she said. *A golf ball? What?*

The day after we brought Palmer home, we had to take her back to the hospital to have her bilirubin levels checked because she had slight jaundice. Bilirubin is a yellow pigment that's in red blood cells; it's common for it to be high in newborns, but if it's too high, in some cases it may indicate an underlying disease. That morning before we went back to the hospital, I took a shower—with Jason's help—and actually blew my hair dry and put on makeup. The whole process was absolutely exhausting, but at the time I think

I was trying to prove something to myself. I always saw photos of women holding their newborns and looking amazing on social media, and I didn't want to roll up to the hospital with Palmer in my arms feeling defeated. This was the last time I put on makeup for a while. (Note to new moms: you don't have anything to prove to anyone. You just had a baby!)

Jason parked as close as he could to the hospital entrance. But I was so weak that I couldn't even walk the hundred feet from the car; he had to push me in a wheelchair. In my opinion, you really should have a handicap placard for at least the first week postpartum. Right? So I was weak and tired and wondering when the heck I'd feel connected to Palmer. *Where's the joyful elation that everyone talks about? The fireworks? The only emotion I'm having is panic.* I was drained and exhausted and mad at Jason because he's the one who got me pregnant. (Hey, I didn't say I was being rational.) I also worried: *What if that connection to her NEVER comes?* I felt so guilty that I kept these feelings to myself.

Then about a week after we were home, I was rocking Palmer to sleep in the glider when she looked up at me. Her eyes met mine. And then . . . she smiled! At that moment, something clicked. A wave of emotions came over me and, believe it or not, I cried. *My heart is not cold and dead after all,* I thought. I know it sounds cheesy, y'all, but it was a genuine overwhelming love that I didn't feel immediately at the hospital. Now, I'm going to sound like the clichéd mom, so roll your eyes if you must, but that connection has evolved ever since, and I fall more in love with her every day.

That said, life was not mommy-blog perfect—and still isn't now that she's older. No, no, no. I never imagined how exhausting the first weeks would be. I saw all of these photos on social media of new moms smiling and holding their babies. Their hair was done with not a strand out of place, their makeup was perfect and they had the most ecstatic looks on their faces. I did NOT feel this way. Or look this way. (I could barely find time to pee; how did they find time to blow-dry their hair? Even the energy to swipe on lip gloss seemed monumental.) I once read a quote by Maria Shriver where she said that "comparing how you feel on the inside (bad) to the way someone else looks on the outside (great) is a losing proposition. It's an impossible standard." Let's just say I was not your "typical" blissful new mom.

One reason was my case of depression after pregnancy, or postpartum depression. We are very aware of the physical changes of becoming pregnant and having a baby, but not so much of the mental changes that occur after we give birth. And if there was one thing I wish I had done more research on before having Palmer, it would have been this: *How will I be affected mentally?* Yes, we know we will gain weight, we might lose hair, our boobs will double in size and our hips will widen . . . but why aren't we prepared for the HORMONES?

I do not think I had a major case of postpartum depression, and upon doing research, I might just have had what they call the baby blues. (Baby blues are short-term mood and emotional changes, while postpartum depression has more severe and long-lasting symptoms, which I'll share shortly.) I never went to see anyone to get it professionally diagnosed, and it never got to the point where I felt like I should be medicated. However, I had many of the classic symptoms: I cried almost every day for six weeks. I felt like my life was over. I felt sad and like I had nothing to look forward to. I felt isolated and bored and bereft of my old life. I missed the spontaneity that I had before I became a mom, because now every day was Groundhog Day. I felt like I'd go crazy if I didn't get out of the house, but I COULDN'T get out of the house. Having Palmer in mid-November, at the height of cold and flu season, made it reckless to go outside with a newborn. Plus, I was breastfeeding (but more on that in the next chapter). I tried to tell myself it was fleeting and that Palmer was going to grow up and someday turn into a self-sufficient asshole teenager, but it didn't help. The depression was so strange because I had this little baby who I would fight a bear for and loved so much that it hurt, yet sometimes I would just hold her and sob. On paper, I had everything I could ask for, but I was still so sad. I felt regret—*why did I do this to my easy life?*—and I had resentment toward Jason—*why can't MEN breastfeed, too?*—because the brunt of the responsibility landed on me. I felt very jealous that Jason got a break every day when he went to work. In fact, I felt like his life improved while mine had done a 180, which was frustrating. He would leave for work the same as he did before, and I was stuck at home alone with an infant.

When I had these feelings, I would tell myself, *Cam! Wake up! There are women who would kill to be in your position.* Of course, this made things even worse, because I felt guilty and petty to be thinking these thoughts. I am an anxious person by nature. I've never been medicated for it, but I probably should be. Typically, I am able to keep my anxiety at bay with a combo of breathing and meditation, but the anxiety that hit me after I gave birth was a whole new beast. It's natural to worry about your baby . . . but I REALLY worried. I was not prepared to be so overprotective of my daughter. You go from having this baby living inside of you where you know they are safe to where all of a sudden they're outside of you and you have such a loss of control. Not so great.

While I was experiencing my bouts of sadness, guilt and more sadness, I did know logically that what I was feeling was not really ME; it was all of the chemical changes taking place in my body. Somewhere deep inside I knew it would pass, and the little I knew about minor cases of postpartum depression was that my feelings were NORMAL. That knowledge came from some research and reading. Also, my mom had some postpartum depression after her pregnancy with me and had always been very open about it, so that helped me understand it as well. Honestly, that's what got me through. Now, when I open up to women and say that I think I experienced this, more often than not they say, "You know what? I think I did, too." And they probably did. According to one study by the Centers for Disease Control (CDC), a whopping one in eight mamas in the United States experiences symptoms of postpartum depression. According to the American Psychiatric Association and the CDC, these symptoms include crying more often than usual, loss of pleasure in things you used to enjoy, eating more than usual or a lot less, anxiety or panic attacks, withdrawing from friends and family members, a sense of numbness or disconnection from your baby or disinterest in him or her, worry or fear that you'll hurt your baby, having other scary thoughts, feelings of guilt that you're a bad mom, feeling worthless, questioning whether or not you'll be able to care for your little one, excessive anger and irritability, mood swings and trouble sleeping or sleeping too much.

An article in the *American Journal of Obstetrics and Gynecology* said that postpartum depression is "underrecognized and under-treated." I agree. This goes right along with my theory that there are actually a lot more women who experience postpartum than we think; most just don't admit it for fear of being stigmatized. And many don't even realize there's a name for what they're feeling. The good news is that the more we talk about it, the more we realize we're not alone. Treatment options include long- or short-term medication and therapy, but other times the depression goes away on its own, like it did for me. After about six weeks, it resolved itself and I felt like I'd snapped out of it. I totally understand that's not the case for everyone, so it's helpful to mention your emotions when you go to your ob-gyn for your six-week checkup. Many doctors ask about your mental state at this appointment, but if your doctor doesn't, just bring it up. You may feel awkward, but it certainly won't be new to them. One important thing to note is that postpartum depression doesn't always happen right after you deliver your bundle of joy. It can appear weeks or even months later. So be on the lookout and get help if you need it. Remember, you are NOT IN ANY WAY alone in this. All of us mamas are right there with you (as is postpartum.net).

I wish I'd heeded my own advice to get help. Trust me, as a mom you need a break. Friends and neighbors offered to come over and watch Palmer—even just to hold her for a few minutes—but I didn't take anyone up on it because I didn't want to be a burden and felt guilty. As I mentioned, I had Palmer in the middle of flu season, so I became a germaphobe and a hermit, afraid to have people over and afraid to take her out those first few weeks. But I was also too caught up in proving that I could do it all, which I think furthered my postpartum depression. What the heck was I thinking? Every single one of the women who reached out to me had children, too. They had been in my shoes. They could have helped and were eager to do so. It truly does take a village to raise a child, and the support needed for mental and physical stability is major. Around the two-month mark, I started allowing my mom to come over and watch Palmer so I could get out for a couple of hours. I made her read a baby care book before Palmer was born—after all, there is a family story about my mom dropping me on my head as a baby—and as of this writing, even though Palmer's a toddler, I still have not let my mother drive her in the car. (Yikes. I know. I know.) Anyway, just being able to get out of the house and go to Target ALONE or sit in the parking lot of T.J.Maxx was like a Bahamas vacation. Sometimes I wouldn't go anywhere. I would just drive around and listen to music. Rap music. With cuss words. (A true rebel. I know.)

Another thing I didn't expect to happen in those early days was that I'd turn into a horrible friend. Having a baby literally changes your brain chemistry. I'm not a scientist, but I swear it's true! I actually read an article about how the matter in your brain physically morphs after cooking a kid. You're so focused on this baby that you forget to focus on a lot of other things. I actually told all of my friends to please just accept the fact that I was going to be a horrible friend for the first few months. Eventually, you find balance and can manage having your own life while being a good mom, but it takes time.

Then, just to get a little superficial here, another surprise to me was that post-pregnancy hair loss is a thing. Yup, it is. I knew the thickness I'd gained while pregnant would subside, but my hair fell out in masses so big they clogged the drain. The Victoria's Secret hair was fun while it lasted, but it was not so fun when I was shedding it like a dog. I really couldn't wear ponytails because you could see the bald spots around the front of my hairline. It was embarrassing! Some of it did grow back, but not all of it. And how about peeing in your pants? I remember the first time I sneezed twice in a row and I legit peed myself enough that I had to change my clothes.

So now for a few new-mom tips: a friend told me about the What to Expect app. You put in your child's birth date and it connects you on message boards with other moms who had their babies within a few days of you. This way you can discuss what is going on with women who are experiencing the same things. I went on this app every day and it made me feel so much less alone. Actually, I still use it to this day. Let me just tell you that this kind of support is everything. It made me feel like I was part of a community of women all striving for the same thing. Then again, here's another note on social media: although it can be a great source of info and comfort when you're a new mom, it can also have one awful side effect: comparison. Try not to let any of those images of perfection or ease make you feel alone in your hardship. You are NOT alone. And it IS hard. You don't have to look like those images. In fact, those people don't look like those images. They've just captured the one minute their breasts aren't gushing milk or they've washed the throw-up out of their hair. It's such a shame that women, especially moms, are pressured now more than ever to live up to this lifestyle that just does not exist. Think about the COVID-19 quarantine. I thought it was so interesting that people posted much, much less. Why? Their lashes weren't on and their hair color was growing out. They couldn't even fake perfection or pretend their lives were oh-so glamorous since we knew everyone was home.

Another tip: get help when registering for baby shower gifts! I registered myself and, looking back, I could have easily gotten away with having *way* fewer baby products. But I had no clue what I was doing and didn't know what stuff I didn't need. For instance, I registered for three different contraptions that you put in a grocery store shopping cart to protect your bundle of joy from germs: one that went across it, one that draped in the seat and one that was like a sling. Guess what? I never ended up using any of them. No cart cover. No sanitation wipe. (Mind you, this was pre–COVID-19.) I also bought a fruit and veggie puree machine. Did I actually think I was going to make my own baby food? *Puh-lease*. Hell no. I had some lofty ambitions. Bottle coolers, multiple baby carriers, gadgets upon gadgets, aromatherapy for the baby . . . OMG. What was I thinking?? I also bought *way* too many button-up onesies. NEVER BUY A BUTTON-UP ONESIE. ZIPPERS ONLY. If you have a button-up onesie on your registry, go delete it now. You will thank me later.

That said, there are a few mama must-haves, because I'm all for products that make your life a little easier. Before Palmer, I had no idea how hard it could be to take a busy baby's temperature, so one of those scanning ear thermometers is a must. Heck, I've used it on my husband, too. Another must is the right swaddler. The point of swaddling is to help your little one feel safe, secure and cozy—sort of mimicking that feeling he or she had in your womb. It's great when it works, but there are various techniques and it can take some practice to get it right. At least for me. Palmer had broken out of every swaddle I'd tried, so when I finally found the one that worked, it made me cry tears of joy. So ask your friends or Google: "best baby swaddle." Oh, and then there's the baby shusher, which helped Palmer get to sleep. Baby gowns were also a fave because I hated undressing her each time I had to change her diaper— especially in the middle of the night when I was trying to be super quiet. Another issue a handy product solved: once I quit breast-feeding and Palmer was drinking formula, it was hard to get her to hold her bottle. This could be annoying if I wanted to feed her but didn't want to have to hold her bottle for her—that was until I found these miraculous little handle grips that you attach to the bottle. It's the small stuff that can make all the difference!

One big thing that was a game changer for me was the glider chair. It's basically the modern version of a rocking chair and I think it is one of the most important purchases you'll make. After all, you will spend a LOT of time in it—feeding, sleeping, rocking and reading. So I sat in many different chairs looking for the perfect one. I felt like Goldilocks trying to find the one that was "just right." I wanted a glider that either reclined or had a gliding ottoman so I could put my feet up in case I wanted to sleep, one that had a high enough back so I could rest my head and one that was wide enough for Palmer and me to sit in side-by-side as she got older because I knew reading together would be very important to me. I went to a few different stores, but the one I ended up buying my chair from actually gave me a life-size newborn doll to hold while trying out the various chairs. This was very helpful because I could get a sense of how comfortable different positions would be in each chair. Now that she's three years old, Palmer and I still sit in the glider to read and talk as part of our nightly routine before bed and, while she's too big to be in my lap anymore, we still can fit!

The bottom line is that having a newborn is draining, but you wouldn't necessarily know thanks to social media and the mythology of motherhood. Maybe moms think that if they talk about how hard it is, they're weak. It's a bit startling when you're knee deep in diapers and poop and breast milk and you realize, *This is my new life. There's no going back. It's no longer about me.* But for me at least, it was a lesson that I needed to learn. Yes, the world used to center around me, but now it doesn't, and I'm shocked to say that a few years into it . . . I'm okay with that!

Motherhood is such a mix of emotions. Your life revolves around this being and you're forced to be unselfish. But you also have this little baby who is part of you and part of your partner and you have unconditional love and will do anything for him or her. I can't think of anything better than that! And as tough as that baby phase is, I'd kind of give anything to go back and relive it, well, just briefly. I think I even knew it at the time. I would love to feel the weight of a sleeping newborn lying on my chest again. I'd love to smell her baby head again (best smell in the world). I would totally go back and get up in the middle of the night again (just once, though) to go rock a baby back to sleep. (This is tough to do with a three-year-old.) It's funny because when you are in the midst of this hard phase, these are the things you take for granted. I remember my mom saying, "Don't rush this phase away, one day you might miss it" . . . and the funny thing is, I do, but I still don't want to do it again. Does that make sense? It might not. A lot of things about motherhood don't make sense. And, in my opinion, that's the beauty of it.

Chapter Eight

ON THE BOOB

Between being CEO of a billion-dollar business I
started in my living room and being a mom, I can
say for SURE being a mom is harder!

—JAMIE KERN LIMA, FOUNDER OF

IT COSMETICS AND MOTHER OF TWO

The hardest part of the first year of motherhood was, well, not being prepared for how hard the first year of motherhood was going to be. Now, let me preface this by saying it is absolutely NOT this way for everyone. Some women have no problem losing sleep. Some women don't have postpartum depression and some women experience very little hormone fluctuation. Some absolutely love having their babies on their boobs. God bless them! For some, it all comes naturally. Or so they say. Well, I ain't going to lie. For me, y'all, it did not come naturally.

One of most unnatural parts was breastfeeding—something I got asked about all the time. Actually, come to think of it, it was one of the top questions I got from EVERYONE while I was pregnant with my buttercup: do you plan on breastfeeding? What is it with people's obsession with how I choose to feed my baby? Even total strangers would ask me this question. Did they just want to start a conversation and think it was an easy icebreaker? It seemed really odd to me at the time and very intrusive. So much so that I addressed it on social media. I responded that I would feed my baby however I saw fit. I wanted other new moms to know that if they weren't able to breastfeed, their babies would be okay!

I had done research on nursing prior to having Palmer and knew two things for sure: for some women it was easy, and for some women it was hard. (I guess like most aspects of motherhood. Actually, most aspects of life.) When I checked into the hospital to have my baby, the nurse asked me, "Bottle or breast?"—meaning, did I plan to nurse or bottle-feed my baby? Like many women, my mode of thinking was, *Breastfeeding is what our bodies were designed to do, so I'm at least going to give it a shot.* The nurse wrote "breast" on my chart. *Um . . . Guess that means I'm committed.*

Within five minutes of Palmer being born, the nurse propped her up on my left boob. *Well, here we go . . . it's D-Day. Is she gonna latch or be a problem feeder?* I thought. *Come on, P, you can do it!* I had zero expectations of what my experience would be like. Luckily, she latched right on and began eating like a champ. The nurses even commented about what a good feeder she was. What I did not know at the time is that it wasn't my milk that she was drinking; it was something called colostrum. This is the first secretion from your boobs after giving birth. It's rich in all the good-for-you protein and important antibodies, which help build your baby's immune system. It also helps the baby's digestive system get off to a good start. Some people call it "liquid gold." It comes out slowly, which is supposedly by design so your bundle of joy can learn how to nurse. I don't know about you, but I'm amazed that the female body is SO immensely smart, strong, intricate and powerful.

Now, we all know that your boobs grow when you get pregnant. I welcomed this change because I had stuffed my bra for the majority of my adult life. My boobs went from an A cup to a C cup with pregnancy alone and I was under the impression that they were as big as they were going to get. Hahahahaha. Boy, was I wrong! What I was not prepared for was my milk to come in three days after delivery (the typical time frame) with a fury. My boobs went from being small C cups to double D's. Yes, D's! In only twenty-four hours. OH MY GOD. I couldn't believe what I saw in the mirror. It was fascinating, shocking and PAINFUL.

I knew that breastfeeding could be difficult and had heard that not making enough milk was a top concern among new moms. That wasn't my problem—*at all*. My issue was one that most women who struggle to breastfeed would die to have: an abundant supply, actually an *oversupply*. I'd never heard of that before, but it's actually a thing—as I was told by a lactation specialist. I was a full-fledged freakin' milkmaid who could feed a third-world country. Good Lord! One day early on, I was nursing Palmer on my right boob and there was milk just gushing out of the left. Jason couldn't believe his eyes. It was insane and not at all glamorous. The fact that I was producing that much milk was kind of crazy because, let's face it, I don't have a healthy diet. I eat like a truck driver—a truck driver who loves Vienna sausages from the gas station—and yet there I was, this endless food source for my child.

Even more surprising was how time-consuming and all-encompassing breastfeeding could be. It became the main focus of my day and night, ALL day and ALL night. And my boobs hurt so badly. When you are breastfeeding, YOU are the only one who can feed your baby. That is, unless you pump and can give a bottle to someone else. That sounds simple enough, but not for me. Thanks to my oversupply issue, too much stimulation just made my boobs produce more milk, so pumping exacerbated the problem and caused my boobs to literally pour milk. It was awful and left me feeling captive and isolated. When you are the only person who can feed your baby 24/7, it's impossible to leave the baby and get anything done. I couldn't run even the simplest errand because if I spent too much time away from Palmer, my breasts would become engorged. This is a fancy way of saying that your boobs become uncomfortably full of milk as well as rock hard and painful. And it happened so quickly that I had to keep Palmer close to me at all times to nurse. No doubt this added to my postpartum depression.

The rare times I did go out without Palmer, I quickly learned that I had this superpower: hearing a baby cry in public made my boobs leak milk. No kidding! And always—*always*—at highly inopportune times. So much so that I could not leave the house without massive amounts of cotton padding in my bra to absorb the leak. But here's how I learned this the hard way. During my first

Target outing alone after Palmer was born (which I swear felt like a frickin' vacation), a baby cried a few aisles over. Oh man. It was like someone released two fire hoses and the milk gushed out of me, all over my clothes for everyone to see. With a cart full of stuff, I had two choices: abandon my potential purchases and my little vacay and go home *or* get in line and pay for my stuff. No surprise, I chose the latter and just went to the checkout, trying to ignore my milk-drenched T-shirt and the awkward looks I received. This was something I got used to, since I began leaking 24/7 and my clothes were constantly stained. To make matters worse, sometimes Palmer choked when I fed her because my milk came out too fast. Imagine being on the receiving end of a fire hose. This is what you call a "forceful let-down," and it's a by-product of having an oversupply.

Desperate to figure out what I could do to remedy my situation before I found myself in a padded room somewhere, I had a breastfeeding consultation at the hospital where Palmer was born. The lactation consultant there gave me some tips on positioning her differently while feeding. One was to nurse her while lying on my side. Well, this just turned out to be very awkward and didn't work. Another tip was to nurse more frequently to reduce the amount of milk that accumulated between feedings. NOPE. I already felt like I was nursing around the clock. I also tried to manually squeeze out milk with my hands. Yes, like milking a cow. (I'm sure this was a sight for Jason.) I had read that the tub was a good place to do it because breast milk is actually good for your skin, so I'd sit in the tub and think I was giving myself a luxurious milk bath. This, too, was short-lived. There were times I would nurse Palmer and just sob and sob and then . . . sob some more. On top of my oversupply, I got mastitis several times. This is an inflammation of the breast tissue and blocked milk ducts that caused aching welts the size of large grapes under my arms, along with intense breast pain. I'd never heard of this before, so the first time I got it, when I had the accompanying fever and chills and felt like death, I thought it was the flu. Regardless, I pressed on with nursing, trying to make it to the three-month mark, because I'd read that the first three months helped reduce your baby's risk of various infections, allergies and diseases.

Sometimes I'd call my mom crying and say, "This is so hard. I can't take it anymore." One day she said, "Cameran, I feel like you're looking for permission from someone to stop. You're miserable. Just quit!" I told you my mama has always had my back! Well, I made it to three months with my baby on the boob, but *barely*. I realized that I couldn't be a good mom to Palmer if I was feeling down mentally, so I made the personal decision to stop. For MY sanity. I know it's controversial, but I'll say it: breastfeeding was awful. For me. Emphasis on ME. I know, I know. Some women love it. Not me. Some say it's the best, most bonding part of their day. Not me. Some women want to do it as long as they can. Not me. I felt like a prisoner. Of course, this was when the guilt set in again. I knew Palmer would be fine, but I still felt bad. After all, it is rammed into your head from the moment you become pregnant that breastfeeding is by far the best thing for your child. So there I was, totally able to breastfeed, making plenty of milk, and I was choosing to stop. But you know what? My mother never breastfed me. I was one of the babies who couldn't do it, so I was bottle-fed from birth and I think I turned out A-okay. (In my not so objective opinion.)

It was an arduous process to wean Palmer and dry up my supply. Stopping breastfeeding cold turkey when you have an oversupply of milk isn't an option. You have to do it slowly so you don't get mastitis, or get it again in my case. IT. WAS. PAINFUL. I started the weaning process by giving Palmer a bottle of formula instead of nursing her for one feeding every three days. Even this small amount wasn't easy. At first, she refused to take the bottle, so I swear I bought about fifteen different types (who knew there were so many?) until I found one she liked. Exhausting! And it's not just going from a real nipple to a bottle nipple that's different for your baby. The baby also has to get used to the formula flavor after months of mama's milk. I tried a few kinds before I found one that Palmer liked. I even tasted my breast milk to be able to compare it. Eventually, I found bottles and formula she liked and continued to slowly replace breastfeeding sessions with bottle feeding.

I also tried all the old tricks said to help dry up your breast milk. I drank sage tea, put cabbage leaves in my bra (yup, you read that correctly, full-on cabbage leaves) and avoided hot showers. The hardest part of weaning was knowing that it was my decision to do this and it wasn't because my supply was dwindling or I had an inability. I probably could have gone on to feed Palmer for a full year—and a few other kids—if I wanted to. But I was making a conscious decision to give up something that is supposed to be natural and something that a lot of women pray they are able to do. It weighed heavily on me. I also knew that once I weaned, there was probably no going back.

Getting a baby who has only had a boob used to a bottle is no easy task, but we did it in two months. And I will never forget what I knew would be our last nursing session. Palmer, wearing a zippered onesie with hearts on it, and I were in her room. It was late in the day with the sun setting outside our window. I sat in my glider chair with my feet propped up on the matching ottoman. I started rocking her back and forth and watched her nurse while I sobbed like a baby and took in the moment. I felt so many emotions over the finality of it all, but I still knew deep in my heart that my mental health was dependent on quitting. I also knew Palmer would be fine.

And then . . . Eureka! Freedom!

I posted on Instagram about my decision to stop even though I knew I was opening up the floodgates by doing so. I wrote: "Today marks the day I am DONE with breastfeeding. Gave it a good almost three months and I am retiring the boobs. Writing this in hopes it will make other mothers feel less alone. You see, I'm not quitting because my milk supply dried up or because I'm sick. I'm quitting because I'm just plain over it. By CHOICE. I know I will get lectured and judged by this, but it doesn't bother me. I need some freedom back for my sanity and the bottle and formula will allow that. You are NOT a bad mother if you don't like breastfeeding. A happy Mama is the best gift you can give your baby. At least in my opinion."

I did receive some negative comments about being selfish and how it wasn't healthy for my child, but I would say the overwhelming majority of the more than 20,000 comments I got were from women who understood. They said, "I felt the same way, but I felt pressured by society to continue breastfeeding even though it was making me depressed" and "Thank you so much. Finally I'm not alone" and "OMG this post just made me feel NORMAL" and "I truly need this post and all the comments." The last one was written by a woman who added that the guilt of stopping was tearing her to pieces and that "I hurt all day, every day." WTF? We are not supposed to hurt all day, every day—especially when we need to take care of our children—and if that's the case, it's okay to stop. (Think men would do anything that hurt all day, every day?) Weeks, months and even a YEAR after I posted that I was quitting, I'd get comments from women saying, "I literally went and searched for this post today" to "help encourage me" or to "reassure myself that it is indeed okay to quit electively." Can you imagine that they had to search for a year-old post just because they wanted to feel the support from another mom who couldn't do it anymore? I'm not sure what this says, but it's clear that the pressure and support to breastfeed is strong. And it might just be too much.

I later read a CDC study that found that most women plan to breastfeed exclusively for at least the first three months, but only one-third of them achieve that, for a variety of reasons. I wish I'd known this back then! For me, the bottom line is this: the mental health of the mother is far more important than the extra nutrition breastfeeding gives the baby (if it's even true that breast milk is more nutritious), and if it's at the expense of your mental health, quit and give your baby formula. Your baby will be okay. Palmer was totally fine, loved formula and grew and gained weight as she should for her age. You will rejoice, despite the fact that your boobs will deflate and look like tea-bag city.

Once Palmer was fully on a bottle, I felt like a weight had been lifted. She was no longer totally reliant on me. When I could finally leave my house for more than two hours, the first place I went was . . . you guessed it: Target. There wasn't really anything I needed; I just wanted to feel like "myself" again. Me, a shopping cart and a Starbucks. It was heaven. Other times I would go for a drive and listen to music in my car . . . music that I would feel bad playing in front of a baby. Living on the edge, I know. I could also sleep through the night without my throbbing boobs waking me up. Mentally, I was in a much better space. Whatever postpartum depression I had was finally going away.

If I could give new moms any advice, it would be this: do what works for YOU. Women, especially in this day and age, should not be ashamed if they can't breastfeed or if they flat-out don't want to. Your mental health, especially as a new mama, is absolutely PARAMOUNT. A happy mama makes a happy baby. If you are not in a good headspace, it's hard to be the best mother you can be. One thing that made me feel better was this post by a group of moms who say they adore their kids but admit motherhood is hard AF: "PSA: If you ended up asking for the epidural, you weren't able to breastfeed and you are keeping your bed to yourself because even a little sleep is the only thing maintaining

your sanity, you are not a failure. You are still a badass mom."
Amen! In my opinion, if you feel that breastfeeding is making
you depressed or stressed, it's okay to stop. FED IS BEST. That's
all that matters. If your baby is fed, you're doing a fabulous job;
the method by which you do it (bottle or breast) isn't all that
important.

Chapter Nine

IF YOU DON'T SNOOZE,
YOU LOSE

I don't want to sleep like a baby.
I want to sleep like my husband.

—UNKNOWN

Sleep. Ahhh, sleep. How we take it for granted in our pre-motherhood days. Maybe I'm just speaking for myself here, but I know I did! I've always been a great sleeper, and pre-pregnancy, I would do it for about nine straight hours every night and wake up bright-eyed and bushy-tailed every morning. My first hint of sleep struggles came during my sixth month of pregnancy. That's when I started waking up around 1 A.M. to pee every single night. I'm convinced this is intelligent design during pregnancy to prepare you for the sleepless nights ahead. Now we all know a Mary Sue whose firstborn slept through the night starting at two weeks old. Well, in my opinion, Mary Sue is full of shit. Maybe she just took Ambien.

As a new mom, sleep is one of the key things that help you manage the unknown, sometimes crazy/sometimes monotonous baby stage. I think exhaustion contributed a lot to my mood and postpartum depression. After all, when you're totally exhausted, your brain is not functioning. Navy SEALs use sleep deprivation as a form of training because it pushes you to your limits. But neither you nor I is a Navy SEAL, so we've got to get our rest. I'm happy to say that despite my new-mom fog, I was aware enough to remember a deal I'd made with myself when I was pregnant: I was not going to be overly crazy about getting up and going to my baby every time she made a peep. The only thing I'd read a lot about prior to having Palmer was sleep training, and I implemented everything I learned right away. Well, almost right away.

I thought I needed to have Palmer in a bassinet directly next to my side of the bed because I was breastfeeding, so that's where she was our first night at home. I had ordered the latest and greatest bassinet, one that vibrated and had a white noise machine built into it. Well, let's just say it was a total waste of $400. I got zero sleep. Palmer was within two feet of me and I heard EVERY. SINGLE. MURMUR she made. My senses were already on high alert, but they went into overdrive with her being so close. She also cried a lot, so I had to get up and go to her several times. This would have been a bit easier if I were able to just bounce up from the bed. But my perineum was being held together with stitches, so just sitting down hurt big-time. I actually had to *roll* out of the bed slowly to get up. After waking up for the third time that night to nurse, I started crying. Jason wanted to be able to help me, bless his heart, but God didn't give him boobs.

I quickly realized it's like this: if you're in the kitchen of your favorite restaurant, you're going to want to eat. I know I would. Palmer could smell me sleeping right beside her, so it was a nonstop feeding frenzy and she never seemed to settle down to sleep. The next morning I looked at Jason and said, "Tonight she's going in her crib." I decided to try the methods suggested in the various books I'd read. The book that helped me the most was *Moms on Call Basic Baby Care*, written by two pediatric nurses with over twenty years of experience and eight children between them. I figured those ladies must know what they're talking about! And they did. This book became my baby bible. The main takeaway in all the sleep books I read was pretty much that your baby will sleep best in a crib. This sounded great, really great, but along with the allure of a full night's sleep came the guilt. *Should I really put my three-day-old baby in a dark room by herself?* I thought. *She was in my safe, warm tummy less than seventy-two hours ago! What if she stops breathing? Will I hear her cry? Will she be scared?* Just the thought of this made me sweat profusely. But when evening came, I swaddled Palmer up and placed her in her crib. I turned on the white noise machine and closed the door behind me. I'll be honest . . . I was very apprehensive, because it felt a bit unnatural for this tiny infant to be in a room down the hallway, but I knew I needed to do it so I could get some sleep. Yet, like most things, there was no need to worry. Palmer did great. It was a much more restful night than the one before—for both of us. *Okay . . . I can do this*, I thought. *I can be strong.*

Well, I'm happy to report that my little bald-headed counterpart has slept in her own room ever since. Clearly, she did better when she moved away from her favorite restaurant. The confidence and satisfaction that gave me was almost worth the money I wasted on the bedside bassinet with all the bells and whistles. I kept a consistent schedule every evening (and still do). Bath, bottle, bed. When she would wake to feed, I would go in the room with the lights down low, trying to be as quiet as possible and not saying a word. I only talked to her if she seemed agitated or needed soothing. Then I'd feed her and put her straight back into her crib. If I needed to do a diaper change, I did so quietly and quickly, which is why easy-access baby gowns are key. To this day, I keep a white noise machine on high in her room. This has worked for us, but of course, to each her own. A lot of women find that it works to have their babies in their beds or rooms, but the moment Palmer went down in that crib for the first time was the moment I started to feel human again.

I'm not saying it's easy. And I think the reason so many women have trouble getting their children to sleep is that they feel guilty about not rushing to them every time the baby makes a peep. Yes, this *is* very hard because we have this weird maternal instinct that wakes us up and takes over, pushing us to check on our baby's every whimper. It's definitely a mama thing, because my peacefully sleeping husband didn't hear Palmer once—and still doesn't. Practically defying biology is the only way that you are going to get rest. And if you are not able to do that you will end up haggard, tired, resentful and pent up. You have to be tough and know that your baby *will* be okay. Soon enough you will learn what this cry means and what that cry means and be able to determine if you really need to go to your child or not. It's hard to explain, but as a mother you start to just instinctively know what different sounds mean. I was able to differentiate a real cry from a dream cry. Sometimes Palmer would let out a cry while she was still asleep, and I could tell that it wasn't anything serious. Of course, the first couple of times she did this I still got up to check, but soon I didn't have to. If she really needed me or was upset, it was a different pitch and pattern of cry. Some women say they feel like bad mothers for not responding to every little cry, when in reality they're being GOOD mothers because—and I always go back to this point—if you are not taking care of yourself and setting boundaries, then you are not going to be the best mom that you can be.

I knew I'd reached a new low when Palmer was about three months old and I was desperate to take a bath. When the tub filled up, the water was brown. Yup, brown and murky. Something was obviously wrong with the pipes, but I was just too tired to care and the hot bath felt oh so, so good. So I just prayed I wouldn't die from the water, closed my eyes and enjoyed the quiet time.

Once Palmer stopped waking to feed and slept through the night at around four months old, it changed my whole life. When Palmer slept through the night, I did, too. I started to think more clearly, have more energy and even *look* more like myself. Finally, I understood what other mothers meant when they would tell me,

"Hang in there—it gets better." It definitely did! I felt like a new woman. Honestly, if you can make it through the first three months with a newborn, you can make it through anything.

At this point when Palmer was sleeping through the night, I tried very hard not to go check on her each time she did wake up and make a noise. This took a lot of willpower because of my motherly instincts, but I knew she needed to learn how to self-soothe (an important skill we all need later in life, too). This is not to say that I left her in the crib all night, every night, but if she did let out a little cry, I would just quickly go pat her on the back and say, "P, you are okay. Go back to sleep." I tried not to pick her up or linger in the room. I truly think this helped Palmer to become a great sleeper.

Here's another thing: Palmer has not slept in our bed once. This was a firm rule we made from the beginning. As an anesthesiologist, one thing Jason is an expert on is SLEEP. He doesn't even allow us to have a television in our room because his opinion—and that of many other sleep experts—is that the bedroom is for two things and two things only: "sleepin' and screwin'." Ha! Now, before anyone sends me any messages, I *know* this is a very controversial topic and there are many mothers/parents who co-sleep with their babies, and if it works for you, great. Some of my friends do this. In hindsight, several have told me they wish they had never started that because it's a nearly impossible habit to break, while others are fine with it. Ladies, that's what makes the world go 'round.

Palmer is now three years old and still sleeps twelve hours a night. She was able to climb out of her crib at about eighteen months old, so at that point I just lowered the mattress all the way

My sister, Cayce, me, and my mom, 1986.
*All photos are courtesy of Cameran Eubanks Wimberly Personal Collection
unless otherwise noted*

Cayce and me, 1987.

First night out in San Diego with my new *Real World* roommates.

Real World roommates in Greece.

Me on Lambeau Field for a Green Bay Packers game with the NFL Network.

Me on top of the Seattle Space Needle for a Seattle Seahawks
game with my NFL Network crew.

Jason and me on our
wedding day.
*Photo courtesy of Virgil
Bunao*

My mom and me on
my wedding day.
*Photo courtesy of Virgil
Bunao*

left: Shep and me at the NBC Upfronts in New York City.
right: Filming on the Charleston Battery.

On the set of *Watch What Happens Live.*

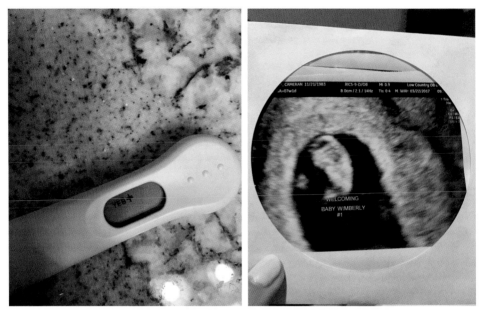

left: The digital pregnancy test that confirmed my suspicion.
right: First ultrasound of a wee baby P at seven weeks pregnant.

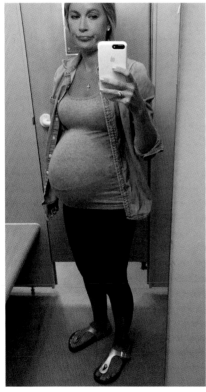

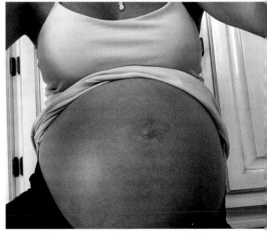

Seven-months-pregnant belly.

Trying on maternity wear at Target.

Eight months pregnant.
Photo courtesy of Kristin Burke

One of our last photos as a family of two.
Photo courtesy of Kristin Burke

Two weeks before I had Palmer, the last time I would get dressed up for a LONG time.

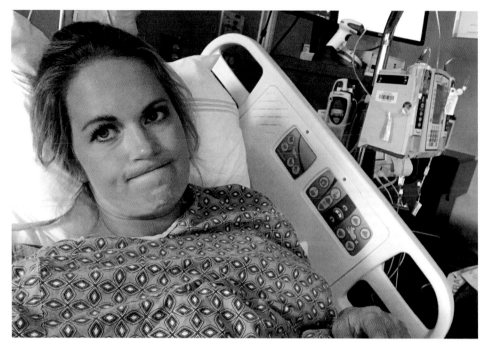

About to check out of the hospital after my failed induction, feeling defeated.

My mother-in-law and mom in the room supporting me, three and a half hours before Palmer was born.

In a daze thirty minutes after having Palmer, wanting to sleep but not wanting to let her go.

First selfie with Palmer! Still hadn't slept.

Busting out of this joint, baby in tow!

At the hospital the morning after I had Palmer to check her bilirubin. I couldn't walk, had to be wheeled.

Week before I had Palmer. Week after I had Palmer.
Whoever said kids don't age you is a liar.

Newborn photo shoot with
two-week-old Palmer.
Photo courtesy of Bump Meet Baby

left: One of many breast-milk-stained T-shirts I would have to change during the day. *right:* The breaking point when I knew I just couldn't breastfeed a day longer. I took this photo because I wanted to remember how I felt.

A sample of the various bottles I tried to get Palmer to take.

Getting the hang. What I woudn't give to hold her like this again!

New mom chic.

Palmer on her first birthday.

My mom walking Palmer to her first
day of school.

My dad and Palmer.
Photo courtesy of Travis Drew

My little ham cracking herself up.

Jason got his fishing buddy!

Palmer and my dad in Edisto
Beach, South Carolina.

Jason, Palmer and Elvis.

Palmer, two and a half years old.

Best feeling in the world!

to the floor to keep her safe. We moved her to a twin bed when she was a few months shy of her third birthday. We really built it up that she was getting a big-girl bed—the kind that princesses sleep in—so the transition was surprisingly easy. (Y'all, it's a miracle!) But let me say this: the decisions that I made regarding Palmer's sleep worked for us. This is not to say that they will work for you. Remember, ultimately you have to do what you deem right for YOUR child. The most important thing is that our children are safe.

Everybody has a different opinion on what to do, how to feed, how to sleep-train, et cetera. If I could give one piece of advice to a first-time mama-to-be it would be this: don't worry. I wasted so much time worrying prior to having Palmer. SO MUCH. I recently heard a quote by Linda Wooten that's so true: "Being a mother is learning about strengths you didn't know you had, and fears you didn't know existed." Yup. And I understand why women say having a second child is such a different experience from having the first, because you are so much more relaxed and sure of yourself. (No, that still doesn't mean I'm having more than one. But we'll discuss that in Chapter 14: One & Done.) When you become a mother, I swear something biological just takes over. Maternal instinct. It's a superpower. Truly. For example, I wasted so many hours researching damn baby monitors. I read many reviews because I thought that I needed one that had good range and reception so I could hear my baby anytime she made a peep. I got one of the top-rated monitors on the market. But the first week I had Palmer home, I quickly realized I really didn't need it at night.

Our bedroom was on one end of the hall and Palmer's on the other, but it was like I all of a sudden had supersonic hearing. Before I had a baby, NOTHING would wake me. I could sleep through a category five hurricane. Not anymore. ANY noise Palmer made I heard, regardless of the monitor. I would sit straight up in bed and Jason would remain soundly asleep.

Whether it's being on the boob or snoozing or anything else, never listen to anyone who tells you something definite about how to parent. There are no definites. There are no one-size-fits-all answers. You have to do what works for YOU. I can tell you what worked for me, but at the end of the day, your baby is not like any other baby that has ever been born and you are not like any other mother.

Chapter Ten

THE SHORTEST & LONGEST
YEAR OF MY LIFE

❧

Being a mom has made me so tired.
And so happy.

—TINA FEY, MOTHER OF TWO

The first year of motherhood was and is a blur to me. It was the shortest AND the longest year of my entire life. When I was in the thick of it, I thought I would never get out. I remember thinking I would never sleep again, that my legs would always have leftover pregnancy cellulite and my energy would always be low.

I never understood why people measured a baby's age in months until I actually had one. It's because SO much changes from month to month, even from week to week and day to day. Palmer started crawling when she was about seven months old. Of course, I was excited about the milestone and the reassurance that she was developing normally. However, I underappreciated the things I could get done before Palmer became mobile. Back then, I could park her in her bouncy chair or on her play mat and she'd stay put. I knew exactly where she was at all times, so if I had to pee or grab something from the kitchen, all was good. But once she could move, it was game over! And when Palmer decided to move, she did it with a fury. It was NONSTOP. That girl was on the go, and no one could get in her way. This made it impossible to do something as simple as make a phone call or pour a glass of juice. What to do? Something I said I would *never* do: I bought what I called the "baby cage," which is one of those white, metal fence-type things that's like a playpen. By the way, I learned that I was a bit judgmental pre-Palmer because there were all these parenting things I *swore* I would not do, and there I was eating crow and doing them gladly . . . actually, desperately. Case in point is the baby cage. I took my stylish coffee table to a consignment store and swapped it for the baby cage in the middle of my living room—actually it took up half my living room because I felt bad putting her in a small one. I filled it with safe toys to keep P entertained—I'd also sworn I'd never let her toys take over the house—and she didn't mind it one bit. Total eyesore? Yes. Stylish? Not at all. But it allowed me to use the bathroom or answer a work email instead of worrying about where Palmer was crawling. Of course, this setup didn't last long. In a few months, her inquisitive little mind learned how to unlatch the door.

Well, if I thought Palmer's crawling was tough to deal with and left me little time to do anything, it didn't compare to her walking. I bought every contraption I could think of to encourage her to walk early. I never put her in a baby walker because I had read that they actually can delay this milestone. Instead, I bought her a balance table and push toys that really seemed to help. Palmer took her first steps a week before her first birthday and was SO proud of herself. (We were lucky to get it all on video, which is huge. Some parents aren't even home when their kids take their first steps.) This is such a huge milestone for a child, and I was filled with emotion when I witnessed it. As happy as I was to see her move upright, it also made me a bit sad because it signified that she was no longer a baby. By Palmer's first birthday party, she was walking everywhere. Now that she was on the go-go-go, I was, too.

One side benefit to Palmer figuring out she could walk was that I finally lost the rest of my baby weight. When the nurse helped me use the bathroom just hours after giving birth to Palmer, I looked down at my stomach for the first time. It was mush. Pure *mush* that made me still look six months pregnant. (I also felt like my insides were going to fall out on the floor, but that's another story.) I immediately lost about fifteen of the thirty-five pounds I'd gained, but that was all baby and water/fluid. The remaining twenty pounds kind of stayed put. I had heard that breastfeeding burns calories, but in my case I think my body hung on to a lot of the weight while I was breastfeeding because it needed it. Truthfully, though, I was so consumed with being a new mom that I really did not have time to worry about my body. I mean, it's not like I was trying to impress anybody. Granted, I gave birth to Palmer in the middle of filming, so yeah, that was a little stressful. But I knew Jason loved me and that was all that mattered, not how well castmates and viewers thought I was rebounding. That said, the summer after I had Palmer, when she was about eight months old, I did not wear a single pair of shorts because I hated the way my legs looked. I think the two hundred Philly cheesesteaks I ate while pregnant contributed to new cellulite that even covered my knees.

After about a year and a half, the weight finally went away on its own, uncoincidentally after Palmer started walking. That's when I never sat down. She quickly learned that walking was boring, and she could get places quicker if she ran. Before I had a child, I remember thinking to myself, *What do stay-at-home moms do all day?* I want to sincerely apologize to my stay-at-home sisters, because now I know *exactly* what you do: you're constantly chasing your toddler. You legit learn how to hold your pee and eat on the go while you follow them around the house. This is why women are so inherently good at multitasking! You can't get through parenthood any other way.

Besides chasing Palmer, I did not do anything special to lose weight. I did not diet, but I did try to walk every day, which I think helped. When I became pregnant, I was already doing weight training with a personal trainer three days a week, and I continued until I was about four months along. I think this helped my body bounce back fairly quickly . . . especially my stomach. Thank God the female body is amazing and very resilient! So post-pregnancy I did about ten minutes of exercises a day in my bedroom to try to replace the cellulite with muscle. I would do body-weight squats at first (nothing crazy—maybe four sets of ten). Once I got a little stronger, I would hold a fifteen-pound weight while doing them.

I also did bicep curls and overhead presses with fifteen-pound arm weights to try to get strength and tone back in my arms. When I remembered, I'd hold a plank, since I knew this was good for your stomach post-pregnancy. I've always liked working with weights because I think you see results the quickest and my body responds well to them. My main goal was gaining my strength back. When I feel strong, I feel GOOD.

During Palmer's first year of life, one of my biggest hurdles was simply "What in the heck do we do all day?" I was fortunate to be in a position to be at home with her 24/7, but filling our days was a challenge, and a lot of the time a little boring. Yes, I said it. I know a lot of women don't want to admit this, but I'm fine with telling it like it is. Let's be real: babies aren't great conversationalists and they are constantly the center of attention, whether you like it or not. When I was pregnant, I told myself that my child would have no screen time until she was two years old. Absolutely no television! *As her mother, I will find ways to enrich and fill her little mind on a consistent basis*, I thought. HAHAHAHA. Yeah, that was short-lived. I let Palmer watch her first TV show as soon as she could sit up, around six months old. Granted, it was *Sesame Street*, not *Keeping Up with the Kardashians*. She watched wide-eyed with wonder while I happily vacuumed the kitchen. It was great. I would be lying if I told you I only let Palmer watch TV occasionally. From the first time she laid eyes on Elmo and Cookie Monster, she more than likely watched TV at least once a day. And guess what? It's fine. Not just fine, but a form of education. (Except when she was sitting with me watching *Maury*.) I'm convinced Palmer learned to count to twenty by twos from watching *Peppa Pig*. You can accuse me of rationalizing her screen time all you want, but this girl can count!

That first year, I also made it a goal to leave the house at least once a day. Getting showered, dressed and ready really helped my mental health. It gave me a focus and made me feel a bit more human and like my old self. We went on lots of stroller walks and on visits to the aquarium, to gardens and to her grandparents' homes. On the days that we didn't leave the house, I had "stations" set up that I would rotate. This included a couple of different play mats with a variety of toys, a piano she could kick, a bouncy chair and an outdoor swing. Other times, we read lots of books. I also made it my mission for Palmer not to get a flat head. Sometimes this can happen if babies are left on their backs for too long, so I was determined to keep her on the move . . . and she owes her perfectly shaped head to her mama. It was part of the reason I was so tired that first year.

Another element of the first year was the newborn pacifier. OH, THE PACI. When she was six months old, I told myself that we would only use the paci until her first birthday. Um . . . then she turned one and I said she would use it until she turned two. Well, here we are at three years old and she still has the paci. I know, I know. I get lots of comments about it when I post pictures of Palmer with a pacifier on social media, but I have to ignore them. (What part of #NoPaciCommentsPlease do people not understand? And why are they getting their britches in a wad over MY kid's paci habit?) We don't use it as much as we did in the past, but it is definitely still a comfort item and I just haven't had it in my heart to take it away totally. It's my fault, but if she still has the paci at four years old, Lord help me. At least I *know* I'll take it away by the time she gets braces.

For a long time I thought my PMS had gotten so much worse after I had Palmer, and I asked friends if they felt the same way. But now I realize it's got nothing to do with that time of the month. It's simply that I'm a mother and my patience is worn thin. Cramps and a headache just seem worse when you are tired and have been chasing a toddler all day. You can't really crawl into bed and binge Netflix like you could pre-pregnancy when you knew your period was about to come. Why? Because once you have a child, your life is not all about you, you, you anymore. And though I'd love to binge on Netflix, I wouldn't trade the exhausting, what-the-heck-am-I-doing life with Palmer for anything.

One thing I *would* trade is the sickness we both experienced the first year. I have always bragged about my immune system. I've only had the flu once and never get colds. Before I had Palmer, I couldn't tell you the last time I threw up. Well . . . enter day care. When she was six months old, Palmer went to a Mother's Morning Out program from 9 A.M. to noon twice a week. Once your child starts preschool or day care, the illnesses begin. Despite the amazing socialization and educational aspects of these places, they are germ factories and there's not a damn thing you can do about it. When your child gets sick, it's likely you will follow suit. Good times. I'll never forget the first time Palmer got sick. File this under The Things They Don't Warn You About. In the middle of the night, I heard a strange noise on the monitor. I woke up immediately and when I looked at the screen, I saw Palmer sitting straight up in her crib. When I got to her room and turned on the light, I saw it. The puke. Lots of it. All over the baby. All over the sheets. All over the crib. The most pitiful sight was poor P, sitting there trembling and confused as to why her body had regurgitated everything from the day before. It was 2 A.M. Jason had to be up at 5:30 A.M. for work, so I didn't want to wake him. I lifted Palmer out of her crib, stripped her down and put her immediately into the tub. Have you ever smelled baby puke? It's PUTRID. I was gagging. She was gagging. We were in this ordeal *together*. Once she was clean (after puking again in the bathtub) and redressed, I then started on the crib. You can't just put a puke-filled sheet in the washing machine. You have to get the chunks of throw-up off it beforehand. So sorry if this is TMI. But at least you can see why I started gagging again. Once I took the sheet off, I realized the puke had soaked through to the mattress, too. *What the f***? How do I clean the damn mattress?* And it was 3 A.M. Mamas, if you are currently pregnant, put a mattress protector on your registry NOW. You'll thank me later. I put a towel down on the mattress and a fresh sheet on top of it so I could put Palmer back to bed. Needless to say, she wasn't down for long before round two of puking commenced. (Counting the bath, I guess it was round three.)

The following day, once the puke was all out of her system, I took the mattress to the dump. There was zero chance I could get the awful smell out of it. I went to Target and bought a new mattress and two waterproof mattress protectors. When I got home I put on one protector, put a sheet on top of that and then *another* mattress protector on top of that and another sheet on top of that. If this fiasco ever happened again, I was armed. I was ready.

The second sickness to hit us was hand, foot and mouth disease. It sounds medieval, right? Hand, foot and mouth is like this generation's chickenpox . . . but worse. The child basically breaks out in these awful sores that ooze and then scab over. And they are all over—you guessed it—their hands, feet and mouth. It's accompanied by a high temperature that makes them miserable. It's also VERY contagious. The doctor assured me it was extremely rare for adults to get it, so I shouldn't worry. Well, I guess I was one of the lucky ones. When it hit me a week later, I literally thought I was dying. (So much for that immune system I used to boast about!) I couldn't walk without being in terrible pain from the sores on my feet. And I couldn't hold a fork because of the sores on my hands. I was bed-bound. I was pitiful. I was dramatic. I looked at Jason at one point and said, "That's it. I'm taking her out of her Mother's Morning Out program!" Another side effect of hand, foot and mouth is that once you are recovered, your fingernails and toenails can fall off. This happened to me, too. Oh, the joys of motherhood!

One thing that really helped me that first year was meditation: the practice of becoming still and calm and clearing the mind of all active thoughts. It is the one tool I have in my arsenal besides sleep that seems to always help alleviate anxiety and stress. Of course, knowing HOW to meditate and actually doing it are two different things; you have to be disciplined. When I was growing up, my mother always meditated. This was something that was not commonplace in Anderson, South Carolina, but my mom was a bit of an outlier in our small town. She would go in her room, close the door and put a sign on it that said "Do Not Disturb, I'm Meditating." As I grew older, I was more and more intrigued about what she was actually doing and eventually read a lot about meditation and started taking classes.

A teacher I went to who was trained in Transcendental Meditation by the Maharishi himself once likened it to the ocean. He said, "Think of your mind like the sea. The surface of the ocean can be turbulent with rough water and waves, but as you dive deeper below the surface it starts to calm itself." It wasn't easy for me to learn how to sit still, but once I did, it was life-changing. Just knowing that I am able to get to that space if I need to is very liberating and greatly eases my anxiety. Labor itself is a type of meditation because it forces you to focus on nothing but the task at hand and your breathing, which makes it good practice for motherhood. When I have the time, I try to meditate—usually in the evening before bed—just to clear my mind for fifteen minutes. It gives me a little recharge for my day. Ideally I would do it every day, but that never happens.

All in all, although it was messy and exhausting and full of lots of unknowns, I wouldn't change a single minute of Palmer's first year—well, maybe besides the puke—for anything.

Chapter Eleven

REGAINING YOUR SENSE OF SELF

Nothing can really prepare you for the sheer overwhelming experience of what it means to become
a mother. It is full of complex emotions of joy,
exhaustion, love, and worry, all mixed together.
Your fundamental identity changes overnight.

—KATE MIDDLETON, MOTHER OF THREE

Palmer and I had been home from the hospital for about six or
seven weeks when I realized that I was tired of seeing myself
in the mirror day after day: a tangled knot in my hair (though I
finally understood the term "mom bun") and no makeup, wearing
Jason's oversized, breast-milk-stained T-shirt and boxers. I would
stare at my reflection and think, *My God, who is this person? What
happened to you?* I also realized that I'd worn my husband's underwear more than my own over the last ten days and that my arm-
pits were on the verge of looking like a man's. It was downright
depressing. So I decided to do what I did before I had Palmer: look
presentable! Imagine that. I made a point to shower every day and

do my makeup and hair, even if I had no intention of leaving my house—and in the beginning I barely left the house, thanks to my oversupply of breast milk. This little thing helped me BIG-time. It seems silly, but when I think I look good, I feel good. And as you know by now, I'm a firm believer that a mother's mental health is everything.

As women, we tend to put our children—and often other people, too—above everything, so much so that we lose ourselves in the process. The key is to remember who you were BEFORE this little being rocked your world and to try to regain that sense of self slowly but surely. Unless you're one of these rare women who want their life to be all about the baby (and if you are, God bless), regaining your sense of self is absolutely paramount to your happiness and well-being. In the beginning, if I went to a friend's house for forty-five minutes or to grab a quick lunch with my *Southern Charm* costars, I felt a little bit guilty being out without my child. But I had to balance being a mother with still having my own life, because babies quickly become the boss and you become their personal assistant. Mamas out there, it's so important to take care of YOU because the best and most important relationship you will ever have is the one with YOURSELF. And if that relationship is solid, you'll have better relationships with everyone else. That in turn makes you a better person and a better mom. It is advice that sounds so simple and obvious, but it's advice that's not always easy to follow.

For me, this emphasis on balance led to the question: should I work or not? My mom has always been my role model, and I can't say enough good things about her and what she taught me. (I pray my daughter looks up to me the same way that I look up to my mother to this day.) Growing up, my mom was not your typical Southern woman. She had my sister and me in her thirties, which back then was a lot older than usual, and after she and my father got divorced, she worked full-time and let my sister and me fend for ourselves. We learned to do our own laundry by the time we could reach the buttons on the washing machine—around seven years old—and we were in charge of folding our clothes and putting them away. We made our own meals and learned how to entertain ourselves. (We lived on about four acres of land in the woods, so it was hard to ever get bored.) As a kid, it was kind of weird, but I'm so thankful because it made me super self-sufficient, something I really want to teach Palmer, too. Because my mother was not a cookie baker or costume maker—and we all know my talents are not in the kitchen or with a sewing machine, either— I always thought I'd follow suit and work full-time, even as a mom. But once Palmer actually arrived, it wasn't as black and white as I assumed it would be.

Growing up in South Carolina, you're taught that you're supposed to get married and pregnant in your twenties and have at least two kids. And if your husband makes a decent enough living to put food on the table, the goal is to stay at home with your children and not work outside the home. These are things that society ingrains in you. But I enjoy working and the freedom that comes along with that. I also don't have a trust fund or "mailbox money," which is passive income from investments, real estate, et cetera that comes to you while you're sitting on the couch playing Nintendo. Since I didn't have any of this, I had to earn my own income before marriage and kids. When I first had Palmer and talked about going back to work, some people said, "Your husband's a doctor. He can take care of you." However true, I was also taught from a young age never to depend on a guy for money. If I learned anything from my parents' divorce, it's that nothing in life is certain. My husband could leave me next week or croak tomorrow, and that's why I think it's important to have your own source of income. Yes, if I didn't work, we would still eat. But I actually like to work because I like to have my own money and I like to feel independent of my husband. We've been married for six years and we still don't have a joint checking account. That's just how I feel comfortable.

There are definitely some women who are born and built to stay at home. They are great at it and that is what they revel in. Good for them! That's just not me. Then there are other women who try to force themselves into that role because that's what they think they are supposed to do. Again, not me. Like many women, I yearn for my own identity, but at first I felt bad about this. It took me time to realize that it's not just okay to want your own identity, it's GREAT. No guilt needed. If working makes you feel like yourself, then you need to do it.

This is why Palmer started that Mother's Morning Out program from 9 A.M. to noon twice a week when she was six months old. It gave me a much-needed break to film *Southern Charm* and do real estate work. Although I wasn't asking anyone their opinions, several people said negative things about this: "She's too young," "She needs to be home" and "You're exposing her to all those germs." And I won't lie: these comments made me pause for a second. But *just* a second. First of all, socializing babies from a young age is super important for their development. Exposing them to germs? The earlier you do it, the better it is for their immune systems. (Mind you, this was before the coronavirus.) I remember Palmer's first ride through Walmart when she was about seven months old. She did it the same way her mama used to: no cart cover and no sanitation wipe, and let me tell you, she chewed that handlebar real good! #ProudMama

Look, I know that I'm lucky. I am privileged. My husband makes a good living and I don't *have* to work, and even though I do, I still have plenty of time to spend with my baby. But there are a lot of women who have no choice, and their babies start full day care when they are three months old. And guess what? Those children will turn out just as fine as those who were home with their mothers, extended relatives or nannies. Actually, they will turn out great, so long as it's what's best for mom and baby.

The first time I dropped Palmer off I cried all the way to the day care, feeling so guilty and thinking, *Oh my God. Here's my little six-month-old baby who is growing and changing every day and I am choosing to spend three hours away from her. What if she does something that I miss? What if she stands up for the first time?* When I dropped her off, she was happy as a clam, but I got in my car, closed the door and sobbed some more. Then I called my mom.

"I feel so bad. I can't believe I'm *choosing* to do this," I cried.

"This is going to be good for her *and* you," my mom reassured me. "It's going to allow you to work and have time for yourself." Mom was right, as always. When I picked Palmer up that afternoon, she was happily playing with all the other babies. She'd had fun and I'd gotten a much-needed break to work and enjoy my regular number-three eight-piece chicken nugget meal with a Coke in silence. After that, I saw dropping Palmer off as my few hours of freedom. (Something I appreciated even more so during coronavirus quarantine, when Jason was working twenty-four-hour shifts and I was home alone with her.)

The truth is that work does not stress me out. If anything, work is a reprieve. Before I had Palmer, I thought that stay-at-home moms had it easy and all this time for themselves. Oh Lord, was I wrong. It's absolutely the COMPLETE opposite. That first year, I felt like I was drowning being home all day with my child. It was mind-numbing, and being at home was not making me be the best mom that I could be. That sounds awful, but I don't care. There were times when I'd count the hours until Jason came home and if it got to be about 6 P.M. and he was not pulling into the drive-way, you'd better believe I was texting him, "Where the heck are you?" I'd be lying if I said that I didn't feel resentment toward him, because being a mom is a job without a paycheck. I'd rather be in an office, because besides making money, you can have stimulating adult conversations. When you're taking care of a baby, you're, well, taking care of a baby. It's not like she was saying, "Thank you" or "I love you, Mommy." When Jason was on call, there were days when I didn't talk to an adult. I felt guilty and awful complaining about it, but I did feel limited.

Here's something else that I learned: women often talk about figuring out how to "have it all" and "find balance." Well, I think that's a bullshit standard. There's absolutely no way to have it all. There's just NOT. We're socially conditioned in this country that when a woman pops out a kid, she has to make the choice whether she's going to stay home or go back to work. And the father is typically, though not all the time, the breadwinner in the house.

But again, it's not that simple or cut-and-dried. I'd worked very hard to get where I was in my real estate career. Actually, I worked hard to find a career in the first place. After not having any direction for a while, I spent three years working as a makeup artist in a department store in Charleston. Then I got my real estate license and briefly joined a woman named Eve, who dealt with some of the most beautiful homes in the area. She offered me a three-month trial period working for her and showed me some of the ropes. After that, I worked with a larger company that was well established in town and worked my way up in the field to become a top seller. Because real estate is a field where you can kind of make your own schedule and that schedule varies week to week, I thought it would be a lot easier to manage work and motherhood. Boy, was I wrong. I worked as a buyers' agent only, so, before Palmer, my days mostly consisted of researching property, running comps, scheduling showings and meeting with potential clients to show houses. Weekends were always a busy time for showing property. In real estate you have to be flexible, and the key word is *available*. This is hard when you have a small child, so when Palmer was born, I had to turn away a lot of clients and refer them to someone else. After being home with her for about six months, I slowly started taking on clients again. (Thank God I had my mom to watch her while I worked.) But I didn't get back in the game the way I was before.

When I was childless, I was a platinum-level Realtor, which means I had sold over a certain dollar sale threshold with my company (around $10 million). The sales levels are silver, gold, platinum and diamond, so I was one step away from the very top. However, the first year after Palmer was born I didn't sell one thing. I went from being on top of my game to forgetting to call back the appraiser! I went from working as much as I wanted to staying home and taking care of a baby. You just have to adapt to your new life and accept the fact that you are always going to have to sacrifice something as a mother. Today, if I wanted a fuller workload I could have it, but I do not take on the same amount that I did before I became a mom. There is always going to be a give, so I'm still working on changing my expectations.

I'm someone who is very goal driven, so it's been hard to shift my mode of thinking from "I'm going to pat myself on the back because I closed this deal" to "I'm going to pat myself on the back because I took Palmer to the children's museum" or "I made her a healthy breakfast." When I talked about this challenge with friends, they said, "Get a nanny," but then I grappled with *that*. (I thought about getting a nanny. I even met with a bunch, but they were all too young and hot. I was looking for one who looked like Mrs. Doubtfire and could change a diaper.) Ideally, I'd like to work and make money all day and then be with my child. But I also know that I'm only going to have one child, so if I get a nanny, am I going to beat myself up for missing this precious time in Palmer's life to sell a house? It's just a total mind f*** either way, and I'm still figuring out the solution.

What I do know is that becoming a mother is simultaneously the hardest and most wonderful thing I've ever done in my life. As much as maintaining a sense of self is insanely important, so is recognizing that you will never be the woman you were before you got pregnant. When you become a mother, the old you is still there, but your identity is suddenly so much more. I saw this quote on an Instagram page I follow (attributed to Lisa T. Shepherd) that said, "In raising my children, I have lost my mind and found my soul." Exactly! For those who say "becoming a mother won't change me". . . well, I hate to break it to you, but it will stretch you, grow you, frustrate you and enlighten you in so many ways.

Chapter Twelve

THE PRESSURE TO GIVE YOUR CHILD (AND YOURSELF) A PINTEREST-WORTHY LIFE

> A mother's love for her child is like nothing else
> in the world. It knows no law, no pity. It dares all
> things and crushes down remorselessly all that
> stands in its path.
> —AGATHA CHRISTIE

There's pressure to be the perfect mom no matter where you live, but I think it's safe to say that the expectation of domestic bliss is heightened in the South. Having a child in the days of social media makes matters even worse. When my mom had me, she read books. But today everyone searches online, reads mom blogs and spends hours on Instagram. This can be great—I got a lot of helpful info from good ol' Google—but going online and on social media also makes it very easy to compare yourself on your worst day to someone else on their most filtered. The result?

It can make you feel like crap. For example, when a mom blogger posted about the baby food she made—yes, *made*—from organic pears, it didn't feel great to know that I was getting Palmer whatever was on sale at Target—buy one jar, get one free. Or when another mom brags about her child never having any junk food while yours is elbow deep in a bag of chips, you may feel like you're not measuring up. Well, guess what? Your kid is probably going to eat McDonald's one day whether you like it or not, so not every morsel you feed the kid as a baby has to be organic.

That said, while I'll never go to great lengths to make pureed vegan baby food, I've fallen into the keeping-up mom trap. I swore to God that I was not going to be one of those moms who throws an elaborate first birthday party. After all, why spend a bunch of money when your baby's not going to remember a single second of it? Total waste. I also felt this way about her first two Christmases. People would ask me what I was getting her and seemed shocked when I said, "Nothing. She has enough." I wasn't being a Scrooge. My point was that Santa would come deliver the goods when Palmer could understand. Also, her birthday is November 11, so she received a ton of presents right before the holidays anyway. I don't want her to be a spoiled child, so I purposely hid a good many of her birthday presents and recycled them as Christmas gifts. Cheap of me? Yes . . . but you gotta admit, it was kind of genius. I stuck to the no-Christmas-gift thing and didn't introduce the Easter Bunny until she was two years old for the same reasons. I figured it was impossible for Palmer to understand the concept of either any earlier. But I was obviously full of shit about the party, because it wasn't the same with the birthday bash. Why? Because I got invited to friends' kids' first birthdays and the guilt set in. So did the comparisons of myself to other moms with parties that were Pinterest-worthy. *Won't I be judged if I don't have a big bash? She's going to be my only baby, so I should have a big party*, I thought. Yup, I found myself totally eating crow on this one and planning a birthday party that was so stressful and time-consuming that it might as well have been her wedding. Okay, not that bad, but you get the point.

I started thinking about it when she was about eight months old and decided on an Elvis theme. Elvis is the fifteen-year-old mutt that forsook our neighbors for us and then became our dog for good when the original owners moved to another state. (It would have been too hard for Jason if the dog had moved, because he and Jason share a deep love.) I even had an outfit custom made for Palmer with Elvis' image embroidered on it and a birthday cake and custom invitations made with Palmer's monogram intertwined with an artist's rendition of Elvis. We had lots of balloons and handmade paper flowers from Etsy. I also invited way too many people, about sixty, and there were six times as many adults as there were children. Family members flew in from as far away as California for the occasion.

I'm not justifying it, per se, but when you become a parent, your whole outlook changes. All of a sudden I wanted to give Palmer a party so she could experience it and we would look back and have memories. I even hired an expensive local caterer. Well, would you believe that by the time the weekend came for the party

I was so flustered and overwhelmed with the details that I totally *forgot* to pick up the food? The party was on a Sunday and the food needed to be picked up on Saturday since the caterer was closed on Sunday. My dumb ass completely forgot. So there we were on Sunday morning with no food. Luckily my friends helped me scramble, and we made do with a local restaurant. We also had a full bar, which in hindsight was a little inappropriate for a first birthday party. Let's just say I had a headache the next day.

Looking back, I am glad I gave Palmer a party. The photos and memories were priceless, and she seemed to really enjoy herself. Of course, then I swore I wouldn't give her a big second birthday party and ate those words also. This time it was a Minnie Mouse–themed party—her first character obsession. Her second birthday was not as involved as the first, but I still invited way too many people. When you become a mama, you do so many things you swore you wouldn't. Here are just a few that I file under Things I Said I'd Never Do: I let Palmer's toys take over my living room and my house. I let her have her pacifier past six months old and I swore I'd never wear matchy-matchy mother-daughter outfits, but just check out my Instagram. Oh well, it's part of the job.

Several of my friends post pics on Instagram of creative meals they make for their kids, making a monkey out of pancakes or arranging fruit in the shape of a funny face. I would see these images and think, *Shit . . . these women have it together. Not only are they making healthy meals, but they are* styling *them as well.* So one time I did this, too . . . but I lied. I can't believe I'm admitting this, but I copy-and-pasted a photo from Pinterest in my Instagram story as if it were my original work. It was a turtle made out of a waffle and apple slices. Is this pathetic? Yes. I did it only because I wanted other women to think I had it together too, and the real truth is Palmer probably ate a hash brown from McDonald's that morning straight from the McD's wrapper!

Even though I won't be styling any meals soon or planning more elaborate birthday parties, I get the impulse. When you become a parent, you intrinsically want your child to have wonderful and memorable experiences. You start to notice how quickly time flies and how fast he or she changes, and you want to do everything in your power to provide for and protect your kid. And, yes, there is a fine line between providing and spoiling, which I try my hardest not to cross. I will never forget the first time Palmer looked at me and her little voice said, "Thank you, Mama." I can't remember what prompted it, but it made me want to cry happy tears. Seeing your child acknowledge something you have done is so gratifying . . . and it makes you want to do more. I will try to keep this memory in the archives if Palmer turns out to be a snotty, rude teenager like I was someday.

And pressure to be the best mama often turns into pressure to be the best-*looking* mama. Another thing I tried to emulate from social media was all the photos of women who wore waist trainers after they had babies. A waist trainer is basically a girdle that you strap around your midsection after giving birth to help shrink your stomach, and these women claimed that it made their stretched-out midsections go back to normal in a matter of weeks. Seems simple enough, right? Not so much. I had the idea that no matter what my stomach looked like after birth, this magical contraption that I spent way too much money on would fix me quickly. I ordered two from different companies and even packed them in my hospital bag. I look back on that and laugh out loud at the fact that I actually thought I would be wearing one in the car home. Truth is, I wasn't even thinking about what my stomach looked like at that point. It was the last thing on my mind. I was more concerned about the blood clots that were coming out when I peed and not falling down from being so weak when I walked.

About two weeks after I had Palmer, I remembered that I had these waist trainers in the closet and decided to strap one on. It's so hard to do that Jason had to help me, and once it was on it felt like a torture device. I couldn't breathe. My ribs hurt. While my stomach looked completely flat under my T-shirt, my insides felt like they were in a vise. This lasted about five, maybe ten minutes, but that was it. I couldn't take it off fast enough and I never put one on again. *Screw this*, I thought. *I'd rather still look five months pregnant.* Instead I decided to embrace my stomach, and although you couldn't really tell this on social media or the show, I would say it took a full year before it went totally back to normal.

Chapter Thirteen

THE TERRIBLE &
NOT-SO-TERRIBLE TWOS

The days are long, but the years are short.
—GRETCHEN RUBIN, MOTHER OF TWO

T he terrible twos started a bit early for us—probably when Palmer was about twenty months old. While it can be a trying time, it is also my favorite so far. Why? One minute Palmer was screaming bloody murder because I wouldn't let her pick up dog poop and the next she was hugging my neck saying, "Luh yew, Mama." Good Lord, did that melt my mama heart! And I get it. I kinda act this way, too, when I have PMS. God bless Jason. But back to the terrible twos. Every stage with a baby/toddler/child is something new, something terrifying and something exciting. At first, I thought the newborn stage was hard. Nope. The toddler stage was harder. That's when Palmer went through a short-lived but irritating phase of slapping me in the face with her hands. One morning, I asked her to give me a kiss and instead she took her little hand and went *whap*.

Palmer is no wilting flower, that's for sure. She is a very strong-willed child. (As was I. My mother tells me this is payback. Ha!) Palmer started asserting herself very early on—even from inside the womb, when she refused to come out until forty-one weeks. She is VERY independent and knows what she wants. If there is a way for her to do something herself, she will try. I hear "No, Mama, let me do it" multiple times a day. If she's sick, she won't even let me be the one to give her Tylenol. SHE insists on sticking the syringe in her mouth and pushing it down to release the medicine. As frustrating as this can be, her independence is also one of my favorite things about her, at least before the teenage years.

Once Palmer officially turned two, she went through a phase where she didn't want to get dressed. She already had opinions on what clothes she wanted to wear, and the only way I could get her dressed in the morning was to give her several choices and let HER be the one to pick out her outfit. It took many tantrums to figure out this trick. One time Palmer straight-up refused to get dressed before a trip to Target. Let me just say that you should never underestimate how physically strong a pissed-off two-year-old can be. I literally couldn't dress her. She wanted to wear a tutu, a diaper and nothing else. She was crying. I was crying. I finally gave in. I put on a hat and pulled it down low and we were on our way. I got a few judgey stares, but I could tell most mothers completely understood. Just a side note to those moms who give you the I've-been-there look when your child has a tantrum in the supermarket, is practically naked (as in wearing a tutu and diaper) or does anything else that's embarrassing in public: thank you. It really makes you feel less alone when you get a sympathetic, I-get-you-girl, this-will-pass nod rather than a what-a-crappy-mom-you-are stare.

On my last nerve, I started to google "toddler refuses to get dressed," and I was stunned when all of these popped up:

toddler refuses to eat
toddler refuses to poop
toddler refuses to nap
toddler refuses to sleep
toddler refuses to wear clothes

Wait, can toddlers really go on poop strikes? Bless their little hearts! At least that put Palmer's refusal to get dressed into perspective.

But while we're on the subject of poop, let's talk about potty training. Who knew it could be so dang hard? As of this writing, Palmer is three years old and she is *still* not fully potty trained. Let's just say it's a work in progress. LOL. Sometimes she will use the potty, sometimes she won't. If she does, I reward her with an M&M. I have probably been a little too lenient with not pushing it more, but I don't want going to the bathroom to be a negative thing.

That said, I reached a point where I wanted to get it done, so I started "potty boot camp." Basically, you quit diapers cold turkey, put your child in underwear and don't leave your house for three days. Yes, it can be kind of a messy option, and I've read that it can make you want to pull your hair out, but supposedly it works. Eventually they get sick of peeing on themselves and give in to the potty. Y'all, I needed you to pray for me during this because it was hell. And I made the terrible/horrible/no good/very bad decision to start it during my PMS week. I bought Peppa Pig panties for Palmer, which I thought she would love because it's one of her favorite shows, but she would just pull them down and say, "Itchy . . . where my diaper?" Let's just say, I cleaned up lots of messes. Palmer would just look at me and say, "I no like the potty" or "I pee-pee in my pants." Then she'd laugh hysterically. Jesus, take the wheel! I gained a newfound appreciation for the expression "pull up your big-girl panties"! She would literally go get me a new diaper and bring the wipes to me when she wanted to be changed. "Mama, I stinky. Get new diaper," she'd say. Yes, I am raising a diva. So we were back in diapers just when I thought we'd be done with them. Oh well. I figure she can't wear diapers to middle school, so eventually we'll get there.

Although Palmer is chatty now, she started talking a little late. It worried me that some children in her preschool class were talking and stringing together words when she wasn't. But other moms assured me she was totally normal and would talk on her own time. And she has. Sure enough, it's like one day a switch was turned on and now she never shuts up. We are in the "what's that" stage right now, so she is constantly asking me about anything and everything.

I have also recently learned what little sponges toddlers really are. They hear and absorb EVERYTHING. Palmer is doing so at a rapid pace and it's fascinating to see what she remembers and learns. Meaning . . . I have to be super careful about what I say around her. I am not a big curser, but I do utter the phrase "oh shit" on a somewhat constant basis. A couple of weeks ago, Palmer was eating her dinner in the high chair and dropped her sippy cup on the floor. She looked down and very casually said, "Oh shit." *Oh shit!* I thought. *She said "Oh shit"!* Jason looked at me and I put my hand over my mouth. I couldn't believe it. WHOOPS. Of course, I was then upset that I didn't catch it on camera. I told her it was a naughty word and to say "Oh nuts" instead. Mom fail. I am trying to replace my tendency to say "Oh shit" with "Oh shoot." I have also had to force myself to stop laughing when she farts on command and says "shew wee" or else, as Jason says, people are going to think she was raised in a barn. Let's pray she doesn't show these special talents in preschool.

One thing I've learned about the second year of motherhood: it's even crazier and busier than the first. Which makes it even more important to make time for yourself. I'm proud to say that, as of this writing, I'm still showering and doing my hair and makeup every day. (Okay, almost every day.) Granted, I have only one kid, but I make sure to find the time each day to get myself ready because it's what makes me feel better. When I feel better, I'm happier, and when I'm happier, I'm generally a better mom. With a toddler, it's very hard to get ready in the bathroom, so I have a little makeup-slash-hair station in my living room where I get ready every morning. This way I can keep my eyes on my child and still make myself look presentable.

Despite the push and pull of this age—the poop, the clothing tantrums and me never being alone in the bathroom—two years old has been my favorite parenting phase so far. I love two because you start to really see their little personalities form. As difficult as Palmer can be, she can also be incredibly sweet. She shows empathy toward animals and other people. She is extremely loving and affectionate. I can already tell that Palmer is going to have a great sense of humor. She is a HAM.

You also start to get feedback that makes you feel not quite so alone. Palmer can tell me she's hungry. She can tell me she is tired or has an upset tummy. I feel like in a lot of ways I have become more relaxed because I'm not solely relying on my intuition. Two is also when Palmer looked at me unprompted and said "I love you" for the first time. Of course, I started bawling when I heard those words. Not gonna lie . . . when that happened I got a pang in my ovaries and a moment of *Ahhh, now I get it*. Palmer will now also run up and hug me when I come back home from somewhere. There is literally no better feeling in the world than to see your child race over to you and put her little arms around your neck. That's the good stuff. It's what sustains us mamas after a long day.

Chapter Fourteen

ONE & DONE

❧

Motherhood can be wonderful
and it can be terrible and all in between.
—MY MOM, MOTHER OF TWO

Are you going for baby number two?" If I had a dollar for every time I've been asked that question, I'd be loaded. People asked me about a second child even before my first bun was out of the oven. They also post on Instagram that I "need to have another baby" or "Your adorable baby isn't a baby anymore! Time for another one?" The answer? No, no and hell no. I have learned to never say never, but I highly doubt I will change my mind. Unless I have a major, MAJOR epiphany or a miracle of God happens, I'm done. For real, 100 percent. I absolutely love, love, love being a mom and am so grateful for the path that led me to Palmer. That said, one is enough, and it's all I can handle. Palmer is now three years old, and the days when she lets me hold her and rock her to sleep singing "You Are My Sunshine" are fewer and farther between. Ain't going to lie, that just kills my mama heart, and it helps me understand why women have lots of babies. But only for a moment.

Motherhood did not come naturally to me. I got flustered very easily with Palmer when she was a baby. Looking back at the first year, I think it's safe to say that I'm not really a "baby person." I wasn't a bad mom; I was just an every-little-thing-irritates-me kind of mom. Would I go back? Yes, but only for brief snippets in time. I would go back to rock a baby to sleep one more time, I would go back and breastfeed once more (just ONCE) and I would go back to smell that newborn head. It's funny how the things that I once cried over (breastfeeding, getting up in the middle of the night) are now the things that I would totally like to know what it feels like to do again. One morning when Palmer was a newborn, after I had been up all night with her, my mom was over. "As crazy as it sounds, you will miss these things one day," she said. I didn't think it was possible at the time, but she was absolutely right. The days are long, but the years are short. That said, if I really wanted to go back to the baby stage, I would have another baby. Today, I enjoy being a mother to a rambunctious toddler who can communicate her wants and needs to me far better than a baby can . . . and I think as she gets even older I will grow to enjoy it even more. It's funny, every month that now passes, I say, "*This*, this is my favorite age, right now."

Once people have a baby in the South, they typically keep going, so the overwhelming majority of parents I know have a minimum of two kids. Growing up, the infrequent times I envisioned myself having children, I saw myself with two. It wasn't until I really got to know myself as an adult that I realized that more than one probably wasn't for me. I think mentally and emotionally, I can't handle more than one, and I don't believe there's anything wrong with saying that. I'm just not meant to mother multiple children. I do not embrace the chaos. I see a lot of women whose kids kind of rule the roost. I'm a control freak, so that is never going to be the case in my house. And the way I see it, Palmer's going to have some trouble staging a takeover all by herself.

My mother repeated *lots* of sayings to me and my sister growing up. The one that she said the most was a quote from Shakespeare that has always stuck with me: "This above all: to thine own self be true." (If I ever were to get a tattoo, it would be this saying.) She taught us that our gut and intuition would serve us very well in life *if* we learned how to listen to them and use them. In this world, we are socially conditioned in almost EVERYTHING, including the biggest and most personal decisions. Get married by thirty, have two kids. The thing is . . . what society deems normal might not necessarily work for YOU. When I would tell people in my twenties and early thirties that I wasn't sure if children were for me, most would look at me like I had two heads. I'm not going to lie; it made me self-conscious. Most would say, "Oh don't worry, you will change your mind." But still, I never let those feelings pressure me into having a baby when I just knew in my gut that I wasn't ready. These people aren't the ones raising your child, so who cares what they say? You don't make a life-altering decision to please other people or society. That's how women end up super bitter.

At this point, I'm in my mama groove. I've got it down as much as I can for being an anxiety-prone woman who struggles to multi-task. (I'm the person who starts a load of laundry only to forget to put it in the dryer. More than once I've had to rewash a load three times to get rid of mildew. Been there, too?) I don't feel confident enough that I could be as good a mother to two children as I am to just one . . . and if that's okay with me, it should be fine with everyone else.

Susan Newman wrote a popular book, *The Case for the Only Child*. In it, she said stopping at one child can be a difficult decision, but it's also becoming a more popular one. Today, nearly 25 percent of families have only one child, a statistic that has doubled since the late 1970s. So clearly, I'm not alone. The bottom line is this: having a child forces you to see humanity and it forces you to grow, and I'm so glad that I did it—but I'm not doing it again. Palmer is now an active little toddler, and she fills up every want or need I felt was lacking in my life. I have someone to love unconditionally and depend on me, I have someone to teach and instill values in, I have a piece of myself and Jason who can carry on our family. I really don't want or need another. Although I think he would be open to having more, Jason is also totally fine with having just one child. Like me, he says his desires to become a parent have all been fulfilled with Palmer and he doesn't have a burning want for another. We do know that there are positives to having a sibling, but we also know there are positives in staying a singleton:

more attention, no competition and more financial benefit. There really is no right or wrong.

Are there times that I wonder what it would be like to have another child? Yes. Most of my friends who were pregnant when I was have already had baby number two and some are currently pregnant. Some were planned pregnancies and others were not. I have one friend who accidently got pregnant when her son was only five months old, so she had two kids under the age of two. She told me she cried when she found out . . . not happy tears, but "I'm scared" tears. The first few months were extremely hard, but now the two children play together and it actually gives her a break. She ended up being grateful to have had her children so close together. Now that Palmer is three years old, I can totally see how a sibling would give me a reprieve from being her constant source of entertainment. On the other hand, I have another friend who knew she wanted two children. She had a boy around the same time I had Palmer and really wanted to try again for a girl. Well, she got pregnant pretty quickly, but with twin boys. So now she has three kids under the age of two. She's tired. *Very* tired.

Now, let me just tell you that I'm writing this in the midst of the COVID-19 pandemic, and there is nothing like a pandemic to bring you closer to your child. It has been extremely hard, and at the same time I feel very thankful to be in a position to be quarantined with Palmer. Her school closed in March, and at one point we weren't sure if it would reopen. Jason has been a frontline worker during all these weeks and months, and the stress has been palpable. I worry about him constantly. I also worry about him exposing Palmer and me to COVID, as he is exposed to it every single day at the hospital. As soon as he comes home, he strips his scrubs off in the garage and immediately takes a shower in our basement before coming upstairs. Due to his high-risk exposure, we have limited who we see during this time. For the first six weeks we didn't see anybody at all, not even our parents. I will say that this pandemic has definitely made me question having another child now that I am Palmer's only source of entertainment. She has developed a very strong imagination lately, so we play make-believe together a lot. I've been a dinosaur, a princess and a puppy dog. To pass the time, we go on "adventure walks" in our neighborhood and hunt for bears. I turn on the irrigation system and let her run wild through the sprinklers. We look for bugs under rocks and for planes in the sky. If she doesn't want to get dressed, I don't make her. We have spent many a day in just a diaper. (Her, not me.) The hardest part is trying to find things to keep an energetic three-year-old occupied and stimulated when you can't go anywhere or see anybody. It. Is. Tough. Not going to lie: she has spent WAY too much time in front of the TV during this pandemic. We have probably seen every movie on Disney Plus. I have actually cried a couple of times because I feel guilty that other children have playmates in their siblings during this and she just has me, a tired mama, but I'm trying and that's all that matters. I'm not going to have another child because of temporary guilt. I know things will get back to normal eventually and playdates will happen again. As with everything in life, I know that this, too, shall pass.

Sure, I would be lying if I said I didn't feel a twinge of jealousy every now and then when a friend has a second baby. After all, they will experience the love and newborn head smell of another child again. (Honestly, I would bottle that fragrance if I could.) But my twinges of jealousy are short-lived when I think about recovering from giving birth, breastfeeding and not sleeping again. Do I feel guilt that Palmer won't have a sibling? Yes. BUT . . . I feel like I'm a pretty good mom to Sweet P. So when people approach me and ask, "When are you going to give that sweet girl a brother or sister?" I respond with, "I'm not. Instead I'm giving her a happy and sane mama."

Chapter Fifteen

GOTTA LOVE THE GRANDPARENTS

The [grandkids] are wonderful,
but the best thing is that you can give them back.
—BEYONCÉ'S MOM, TINA KNOWLES-LAWSON, MOTHER
OF TWO AND GRANDMOTHER OF FOUR

Palmer is the first grandchild for my parents, so one of the most amazing things about becoming a mom—and one I didn't think about—was watching my parents become grandparents. I had no idea how it would change them, deepen my own relationships with them and give me a new perspective on them, but it did. I have always been super close with my mom. She's always had my back, always supported any decision I made without being judgmental (like my going on reality TV . . . twice) and taught me that "this, too, shall pass," which can be applied to so many situations and has gotten me through *a lot* of tough times, from breakups to baby blues.

Becoming a mother has made me see my own mother in an entirely different light. Did she have her misgivings as a parent? Yes. She was never a Suzy Homemaker. We didn't bake cookies and our house wasn't decorated for every holiday. She was never the class mom and our hair was never braided and she could become overwhelmed easily. But these things were *far, far* overshadowed by what she did for us in terms of teaching us to be emotionally well-rounded humans. The life advice she imparted to me has been priceless. My mom is one of the wisest people I know. As an adult, I am able to look back at the way she raised us with extreme gratitude. She has shown me that instilling morals, values and a sense of self in a child is WAY more important as a mother than throwing the perfect Pinterest-worthy party. She has taught me that at the end of the day our integrity is all we really have, and it is the most important aspect of being a person.

When interviewing for *The Real World*, it hit me how instrumental my mother had been in helping me develop confidence and self-worth, but this is something I continue to appreciate the older I get and especially after becoming a mom. Besides her words, my mother has taught me through her own actions how to be a better person. For example, I *never* witnessed my mother gossiping or speaking an ill word about another human being. She used to always tell me, "What Susie says of Sally says more of Susie than of Sally. Remember that." If I meet someone new who has a tendency to gossip, a lightbulb goes off and I think, *Shit, if they are gossiping to me, they will probably gossip* about *me.* Y'all know us Southern women have a predisposition to gossip . . . myself included, but now that I'm a mom, I think of my own mother and I really am trying my best to gossip less. It's ugly, it's mean and it serves no purpose.

My mom also taught us that you should never kill a living thing that isn't harming you in any way. I almost forgot this the other day when we had a roach in the kitchen and I yelled at Palmer to get back. I went to grab something heavy to kill it with and then had a flashback to my own childhood, where I never witnessed my mom kill any living creature . . . including a roach. So instead of squishing its guts in front of Palmer, I got a Tupperware container and placed it over the bug, slid a piece of paper underneath and released it safely outside. Palmer watched all of this wide-eyed. When I came back inside, I told her the same thing my mom would tell me as a kid: "Palmer, you should never kill a living thing that isn't harming you in any way." *This* is the stuff that matters as a mom. These are the things that will stick with a child for life.

One more thing my mom taught me that I hope to pass on to Palmer is the ability to be open-minded, something we need more than ever in this crazy world! I was christened in the Methodist church, and our family went there until I was in early grammar school, but we were never raised to be religious. Instead, we were exposed to multiple religions and spiritual belief systems and encouraged to make up our own minds as to what we felt to be true pertaining to God. This was not the norm in Anderson, but I am so grateful to have been raised this way. I have kept an open mind as a result and do not judge people based on what they believe as long as it doesn't hurt others.

I also have a lot of forgiveness for the times my mom became overwhelmed. Maybe she raised her voice at us more than she should have, but I think back to the fact that she was raising two children under two years old at one point and how stressful that must have been. Children can be wonderful . . . but they can also be incredibly stressful. I get it now. Boy, do I get it!

My mom is the quintessential Southern grandma who lets the kid run the show. Palmer can do NO wrong in Nonnie's eyes. If Palmer wants cookies for lunch, she gets them with Nonnie. If Palmer wants to go jump in the mud, Nonnie lets her. My mom is also convinced that Palmer is the most highly advanced child to ever walk the face of the Earth and determined when Palmer was just over two years old that she has the makings of a nuclear physicist. She dotes on Palmer, spoils Palmer, and loves Palmer to the MAX. Palmer lets out the highest-pitched happy squeal when she sees my mom. I am so blessed that my mom is constantly teaching her and showing her things. Whenever she comes over, she fills up her purse with "trinkets" for Palmer to pull out and learn about.

Then there is my dad. When I found out I was pregnant, he was living more than 1,700 miles away in Denver, Colorado, with his girlfriend of over ten years. Because of the distance, we saw him only once, maybe twice a year. It definitely wasn't ideal, especially with a grandchild on the way. Well, to my surprise, a few months into my pregnancy, I got a call from my dad.

"Guess what?" he said. "I've made a decision: I'm moving back to South Carolina!"

"WHAT?" I replied, ecstatic but also in total shock. I couldn't believe that my dad was leaving someone he had been with for so long to move closer to me. I think my becoming pregnant was a real eye-opener for him. He knew living across the country would make it very difficult for him to forge a close relationship with a grandchild. Besides the chance to be near his granddaughter and watch her grow up, my dad's family had had a beach house at Isle of Palms when he was a kid and I think he always longed to be in the low country. This was the perfect reason to do so. He moved back to South Carolina when Palmer was a little over a month old. Seeing him as a grandfather has been such a joy. He is so wonderful with her and very involved. He's probably put together every contraption and toy I've bought for Palmer and even helps us with yard work due to Jason's crazy schedule. I can always count on him to be there for me. Palmer thinks the world of her "PaPa" and loves him dearly. She is always asking to "go see PaPa." My dad is such a great example of "it's never too late to get it right." I went from seeing him a couple of times a year to now multiple times a week. Palmer has brought us much closer together. Having my dad only ten minutes from my house has been such a blessing.

Palmer also has a bonus grandpa in Mark, who is my mom's partner of over ten years. He is a cowboy-boot-wearing, motorcycle-riding former district attorney from upstate New York. He and my mom are polar opposites in so many ways, but they have one of the best relationships of any couple I've ever seen. Palmer has turned Mark into a real softy. He's awesome, and she is a lucky girl. Mark wrote Palmer the sweetest, most moving letter when she was born (see below). I read it aloud to her in the hospital and it got me so emotional, I started to cry happy tears.

Then, of course, there are Jason's parents, who already had a good bit of experience, having had six grandchildren prior to Palmer. (We call Palmer the caboose of the cousins.) Palmer calls them Doc and Mimi, and both have played an incredible role in her life so far. Jason's dad, who was a family practitioner for forty-six years before retiring, is the grandpa who makes Palmer laugh constantly with funny faces, and Jason's mom, Mimi, is the rock I can always count on. All my worries go away when Mimi is watching Palmer. I trust her 100 percent. She is a nurse by trade and we call her the baby whisperer. I actually ask her for medical advice on Palmer before I do Jason. She is one of the smartest women I know. I am also thankful to both of Jason's parents for instilling such a wonderful moral compass in him that I hope will continue on in Palmer.

All in all, I know that Palmer, Jason and I are VERY lucky that she has five amazing grandparents who love her dearly.

Letter from Mark to Palmer:

Happy Birthday, Palmer,

Today you are at the beginning of a magical journey that we call Life. That journey has no limits other than those of your imagination. You will discover literature, some of which you will like a lot and some of which you might not. But at least try to explore it all because there might be some surprises. There is music, and again try to explore it all because some is amazing. Classical and jazz, rock and reggae, folk and gospel and more. And there are movies, which can offer hours of escape and enjoyment. Perhaps best of all is travel. When they say the world is your oyster, they are not exaggerating. There are wonders around the corner and halfway around the world. There are sights and places to go and people to meet that you will remember for many years.

You do not have to partake of this journey entirely on your own. You have been blessed with a mother and father who are exceptional people. They are smart and funny and kind and gentle and they will always be there for you with their unconditional love. And you also have grandparents and aunts and uncles to teach and show you even more. There are friends you are going to make who will also enrich your life. Some of them you will have for a lifetime. And you will fall in love with your soulmate and have someone to share your magical journey with.

As you grow, you may make mistakes. Everybody does. It is part of learning. Try not to make the same ones twice. And there may be stumbles, but be strong and pick yourself up and continue on. If you need to, get help from your family or friends. They will welcome the opportunity. Be willing to do the same. Others need help, too, and one of the best feelings in life is helping another.

Many have offered words to live by. One group wanted its members to be "trustworthy, loyal, helpful, friendly, courteous,

kind, obedient, cheerful, thrifty, brave, clean and reverent."
Probably not bad at all to strive for. But follow your own mind
and heart.

You will learn about a group called the Beatles. They are
worth a listen. Especially a song called "All You Need Is Love."
Maybe it is not all you need, but it is a good start.

—Mark

Chapter Sixteen

SOUTHERN CHARMING

When my kids are happy, I am happy.
— KRIS JENNER, MOTHER OF SIX
AND GRANDMOTHER OF TEN

W hitney Sudler-Smith originally pitched the idea for a
show called *Southern Gentlemen* to Bravo. It featured an
all-male ensemble cast and the concept was to show the escapades
of their aristocratic lives living in Charleston. The show name was
later changed to *Southern Charm*. Apparently, Bravo loved the concept but felt it needed some female input and perspective. That's
when Whitney approached me. I knew Whitney from the social
scene in Charleston. (I honestly can't remember the first time I met
him. It might have been at a polo match.) He knew I had been on
reality TV before and might be a good fit as a "voice of reason."
But I had a lot of trepidation about committing to another show.

What would people think of me? Would I look like a professional reality TV star? That was not something I wanted. I had been on *The Real World* at nineteen years old; should I do another show at twenty-nine? Also, I had finally become anonymous again, except for once in a blue moon when a random person would interrupt my dinner and say, "Hey, are you that girl from *The Real World*?" Another reason I hesitated: I had been dating Jason for about two years at the time and I didn't want to do anything that would jeopardize our relationship.

I talked to my mom about it and she was very supportive. Even though she doesn't have cable TV, so I don't think she'd even heard of Bravo before, she loved the concept and thought it would be a huge success. Jason was also supportive. So after a lot of thought, weighing the pros and cons, I decided to go for it. My experience on *The Real World* was very positive, so I didn't want my fear to get in the way. *This could be a fun opportunity*, I thought. *And it probably won't last more than one season anyway.* (Of course, what I thought would be one season turned into six for me.)

At the time, I was working at a local boutique department store called Gwynn's of Mount Pleasant as a makeup artist, managing the cosmetics department. I'd been there for three years, working Tuesday through Saturday from 9:30 A.M. to either 6 or 7 P.M. With Jason's crazy hospital hours, we hardly saw each other, so I was ready for a career change. Plus, I knew I could never film the show working those hours. It seemed like the perfect time to make the transition to selling real estate. It was something I'd always thought about doing, but I had never lived in one place long enough to begin as a career. I love architecture and the historical aspect of homes in Charleston, so real estate there was a natural fit for me. When season one began, I started real estate school, and by the time we filmed the last episode, I'd aced my real estate exam and gotten my license. My goal was to go from selling lipsticks to selling million-dollar homes, but I was nervous because I'd quit a job with a steady stream of income and a paycheck every two weeks. Some of the people in the cast grew up knowing that a certain amount of money would be in the bank for them by a specific age, but that's not the hand of cards that I was dealt. Once I got my license, I then needed to find someone to sell a house to! When I told my mom I was nervous about this new career, her response was, "Things fall into place. They don't happen if they're not meant to be." True, but my fear was that if they were not meant to be, I'd be broke. Trying to get my real estate career off the ground made it a little tricky to film a show where I had to go out and be social. In order to pass the state real estate exam, I had to do a lot of studying. That and selling homes were definitely my priorities over going out for drinks every night and being hung over—especially since I'm such a lightweight with alcohol. After all, I have always had the realistic attitude that 99.9 percent of the time reality television is NOT a career. It can be very fleeting, and I always felt it was important to have another means of income besides the show.

Even after my real estate career was thriving, I was still long gone during any filming that was done past 10 P.M. through most of the seasons of *Southern Charm*. I always tried to be honest about what was going on in my actual life, and early on, I made it clear to the producers that I don't stay out late partying. That just isn't in my personality. I did enough of that in my early twenties, and by thirty years old I was just over it. My mom always said, "Nothing good ever happens after midnight," and some of the craziest stuff on the show was proof that she was right.

When I signed my contract for season one, the cast was me, Whitney, Thomas Ravenel, Jenna King, Shep Rose and Craig Conover. (Kathryn Dennis and Danni Baird also appeared in a few episodes.) I knew Thomas socially and had partied with Jenna a lot in my twenties. She was one of the few people who could get me to stay out late. I had met Shep out and about before, but I had never met Craig. One night Craig, Shep and I made plans to have dinner downtown to talk about what we were getting ourselves into. *Gosh, I hope I like these people*, I thought on my way to the restaurant. Within five minutes, I knew that the show would probably take off. Both Shep and Craig had that TV "it factor." They were both good-looking and tall (a rarity in Charleston), with charismatic and gregarious personalities. Although Shep talked on the phone for half the meal, I liked them both instantly. They also split the check and didn't make me pay, which I thought was super nice. We left the dinner with an attitude of *Well, here goes nothing!*

When the show first aired, the local papers trashed us and we got some negative feedback from people in Charleston. I think some worried that we'd negatively portray a city that is supposed to be full of Southern gentility. During season one, it was actually very hard to get businesses and restaurants to allow us to film. It seemed like a lot of people wanted no association with "The Show." Funny, because once *Southern Charm* started taking off, the same businesses and restaurants really wanted us to film there.

When you film, it's important that you never wear the same outfit twice or else it could be confusing to the timeline of events on the show. So for the first couple of seasons when I didn't have a lot of money, I got the majority of my clothes from consignment stores around town. I would find expensive stuff for a quarter of the price. I've always been a bargain shopper when it comes to clothes because I prefer to spend my money on shoes and accessories that can be worn over and over again. The majority of the dresses that I wore to parties and balls were actually from Rent the Runway—though not the one I wore when we filmed the Carolina Day Ball. That was actually a vintage gown of my mother-in-law's from the 1980s. Nobody knew it was old and I got tons of compliments.

When I was on *The Real World,* I learned pretty quickly that too much alcohol and a camera taping your every move wasn't necessarily a smart combo. I have a buzz after one beer and I'm feeling pretty good after two glasses of wine. Give me a shot of liquor and I'm not quite walking straight. I'm not a mean or obnoxious drunk, but I do lose some inhibition. When I started filming *Southern Charm,* I did not want to portray a bad version of myself. The easiest way to prevent this was to have a self-imposed two-drink maximum rule. I actually encouraged my costars to do the same, but it fell on deaf ears . . . about four times in the course of six years

I got drunk on camera and I'm fairly certain I fell down in every scene. (I'm surprised they never did a montage of those clips.) One was a party at Patricia Altschul's house where I lost my balance and fell backwards into her boxwood bush. Shep had to help lift me out, because I was literally stuck in the bush. Patricia hires people to keep her boxwoods impeccably manicured and I felt bad that I'd ruined a couple of them. Another time was my thirty-fifth birthday party. It was an oyster roast in my backyard that was filmed during season six. I was a new mom and hadn't had a buzz in a LONG time. I just wanted to let loose, so I thought, *Screw the two-drink rule.* I got more than a buzz, though—you actually see me falling down onto the grass in that episode not once but twice. Yup. Not that pretty to watch.

Reality TV is like a mirror. If you are an asshole, it will show you being an asshole. If you are kind, it will show you being kind. Being on *Southern Charm* showed me two negative things about my personality: First, I have a tendency to be sarcastic to a fault. Sometimes I take a joke too far and hurt others' feelings in the process. This was something I noticed when watching the show, and now I try to be very cognizant of thinking before I say something that could upset someone. The other thing is that I hate my voice. I don't know why, but I just can't stand hearing myself talk on TV.

Besides that, I got a lot out of the show—especially some amazing and special friendships. Thanks to filming the show, I got close and remained close with the original cast members—Shep, Craig,

Whitney and also Patricia. We were there since the beginning and felt like it was something we'd created and started together. Plus, it's a unique experience that you can only understand if you are a part of it. My role was to be kind of a sounding board/voice of reason for the guys. A Wendy amongst the Peter Pans if you will. I gave it to the guys like I saw it, but I tried to always do it in a lighthearted manner. I saw them as my brothers, and I still think of them that way. One of the people I'm closest to is Whitney. Although we grew up very differently—I'm just a girl from Anderson, South Carolina, who didn't have butlers and nannies, while Whitney came from a much wealthier family with ties to society—we still really relate to each other. We both have a kind of twisted and unique sense of humor that many don't understand. I have cried real tears laughing with Whitney because he is one of the funniest people I know. He is also incredibly smart and well-read and has had a very interesting life. I could listen to his stories for hours. And sometimes I actually do, since we talk almost every day. He will call and have conversations with me like I'm one of his guy friends. Sometimes I'm like, "Whoa, whoa, whoa, Whitney . . . I didn't need to hear all that," but we are just that comfortable with each other. We also share a tendency to be anxiety-prone control freaks. We were kind of partners in crime while filming *Southern Charm*. The good news is that Jason loves Whitney just as much as I do.

Chelsea Meissner is the other person I'm closest to on the show. We were roommates when I was dating Jason and have known each other a long time. When the producers were looking for another female cast member, I thought she would be a great fit. She is a spitfire and like me had been on another reality show, *Survivor*. In fact, she was one of the last three remaining in season twenty-four and almost won. She actually caught a chicken by the neck on *Survivor*, so I knew she would be able to hold her own with the men on *Southern Charm*. I introduced her at a dinner party we filmed at my house and my intention was to set her up with Shep, but she ended up hitting it off with Austen. I was so happy when they added her as an official cast member. She is honestly one of the best people I know. She is selfless, kind, extremely hardworking, not to mention beautiful . . . but totally unaware of how gorgeous she actually is. There is not an air about her; she is just a good and solid person. What you see is what you get, and I love her for that. Jason gets his hair cut by her and I always joke with him that he just wants to go look at her. (I mean, I really wouldn't blame him.) She is the type of friend who I can totally be my silly self around, and we laugh nonstop. I love her dearly. I also am still very close to Shep and Craig and talk to them at least once a week. Shep calls me for girl advice all the time. I feel honored that he actually listens to me, because Shep doesn't listen to many people. Craig and I argue and fight nonstop, but we still consider each other close friends.

The first time viewers knew about Jason was during the second season. I didn't mention him during season one because I honestly didn't believe the show would make it to season two. In fact, I think Jason asked me not to mention him! But from the moment I did, people wondered why he wasn't on the show. Everyone thought he didn't appear because he didn't approve of it or didn't like my castmates. That is simply not true. Jason was and is actually friends with most of them—AND he was the one who encouraged me to do *Southern Charm* each season. But Jason is a very private person and not everyone wants to be on TV. When people asked me about it, I would joke that Jason is just a normal person and normal people don't want to be in the spotlight. Does this mean I am calling myself crazy? Absolutely. We all have a bit of an ego. But Jason doesn't seem to have one, which is part of the reason I love him so much. However, Jason did film the last scene we did on season six (my final season). I think he was a little curious to see how the whole process happened, because the day before he said, "Why don't I just come with you?" It was a party, so I knew it wouldn't be anything too deep or drama-filled and would be nothing more than one scene. I figured, *Why not? Let's do it.* So Jason came with me. He did refuse to wear a microphone, though.

Besides keeping Jason off *Southern Charm*, I wasn't sure if I should keep motherhood off the show, too. I found out I was pregnant before season five, and when we began filming I was already seven months pregnant. I was on the fence about even doing the show, because having a healthy and stress-free pregnancy was so important to me. Jason was actually the one to convince me to do it. He said, "Cam, you can be honest about your experience and it might help other women going through the same thing." This made a lot of sense to me, and there wound up being several parts of being pregnant on television that were very positive. First, I have a little documentary of the end of my pregnancy that I can always look back on. I hope Palmer thinks it's cool someday and isn't totally mortified. That said, when I decided to move forward with filming, I had two caveats: the birth would not be filmed. Of course, production really wanted to film it and my experience, but I just could not imagine having a camera crew in my hospital room. I was barely okay with the idea of Jason seeing a baby emerge from my nether regions. Plus, I did not want any distractions for the doctors in case something went wrong and I needed an emergency C-section. The second caveat was that I would be given at least two weeks camera free after the birth. I knew how important and emotionally delicate the first couple of weeks home with Palmer would be, and I really wanted to have that time privately to bond with her and adjust to becoming a new mother. After a few weeks, I was actually ready to get back to filming and looked forward to it. It gave me a reprieve from being at home with an infant all day. Since I was breastfeeding, though, I could never film without her for more than two hours at a time. My boobs would literally start leaking and I would have to say, "Um, sorry, guys, I have to go now."

Filming *Southern Charm* late in my pregnancy was difficult. I was tired, on edge and really had no desire to party or be out late like the rest of the cast. Luckily, the cast and production crew totally understood and did everything in their power to accommodate me. I think production was kind of scared that making me upset could push me into early labor, and they needed me to be around as long as possible to film. LOL. One night, we had a big dinner at Shep's house that was supposed to begin at 6 P.M.

Little-known fact . . . nothing is EVER on time when you have to deal with a full cast and camera crew. I was always the notoriously early/on-time one. It became a running joke. Anyway, I got to Shep's house at 6 P.M. expecting to eat shortly thereafter. I was nine months pregnant and ravenous. Dinner didn't start until about 9 P.M. and about thirty minutes prior, I went to one of the producers and said, "Look, if we don't eat soon I'm leaving. I have a fully cooked human inside of me." We finally all sat down, and I don't think I contributed one word to the conversation because I was too busy shoving food in my face.

Another cool thing about doing *Southern Charm* was some of the events the cast got to attend. One was BravoCon, which took place for the first time in November of 2019. This three-day convention in New York City featured seventy to eighty cast members from various Bravo shows like *The Real Housewives* of New York, Beverly Hills, Atlanta and New Jersey; *Vanderpump Rules*; *Married to Medicine*; *Shahs of Sunset*; *Top Chef*; *Project Runway* and *Below Deck* in addition to *Southern Charm*, and it was insane. I could not *believe* how many amazing fans came out to see us. I do not see people on reality TV as "celebrities," and to think of myself as one makes me squirm. But people stood in line for hours to get a picture with us and it really felt like an out-of-body experience. A couple of women told me they named their babies after me and I thought, *Oh my God, WHY?* It was a very cool experience to feel so much love and see people of all ages and from all walks of life who adored the show. There was everyone from an eighty-two-year-old man named Fred who told me he never missed an episode to a precious eight-year-old girl. (Although I did tell her mother, "She shouldn't be watching this show.") It was also cool to meet so many of the other Bravo talent who I had seen on TV. Some were just like I imagined they would be and some were complete assholes. I won't name names, but let's just say I was very disappointed by some of their behavior. I watched a couple of the real housewives act as if they were legitimately A-list celebrities. The nicest housewives were Denise Richards and Teddi Mellencamp, and the nicest cast was from *Million Dollar Listing*.

BravoCon made me see how much reality TV has changed since my time on *The Real World*. Besides the number of shows and fans, one thing that's different is that we're in the age of social media, which is a double-edged sword. In one sense it's great, because it gives you a platform and you can instantly reach many people with just one post. On the other hand, it can totally consume you with negativity if you let it and, if you have a public account, people can direct message you anything. I was the last cast member on *Southern Charm* to make my Instagram public. It was private for SO long, and I allowed only close friends and family to follow me. But it came time as a public figure to make it accessible. It comes with the territory. So does the criticism. Around season four of the show, a woman commented on one of my pictures and said, "How can you be married to a doctor and not be able to afford to fix your teeth?" Can you imagine writing that to a total stranger? It actually made me cry and is a comment that I will never forget. I had braces as a kid, but my bottom teeth had shifted. It never bothered me until I read that comment. I couldn't get it out of my mind and I let it get to me. So much so that I actually went to see a cosmetic dentist to get Invisalign to fix my teeth. Yes, that comment cost me $6,600.

Besides that, I have always tried to have a no-nonsense approach to social media. I don't delete comments and I don't block people who say nasty things. In America we have freedom of speech, and quite frankly this is what I signed up for. You have to develop a thick skin. If you expect to go on national television portraying no one other than yourself, there are inevitably going to be people who don't like you. And that's okay. I try not to take offense at it. There are people on TV who I don't like, either (though I'd never tell them that on social media). Yes, negative comments or messages can hurt, but I try to take a step back when I read them and see where the other person is coming from. Sometimes the comments can be warranted. My mantra with social media if you are on a reality show: You don't like the heat? Get out of the kitchen.

Well, get out of the kitchen is exactly what I did after season six. At that point, I had a child and since becoming a mother, my priorities had changed. I also felt like I was at a different place in my life and I just didn't fit on the show anymore. It was time to move on. (My mom always said it was smart to leave the party early.) Also, as a society it seems like we are shocked by very little these days. We've become numb. Of course, it's natural to be intrigued by dramatic situations . . . but the drama on reality TV lately has taken a dark turn and become something I don't want to associate myself with anymore. False accusations can be made and nasty rumors can be started for the sake of a "good show." It just started to feel a bit icky. That said, all in all, *Southern Charm* was a very positive experience. I would go back and do it all over again.

As far as what is next for me in life, I have no idea. Currently I am primarily focused on being a mom. Real estate has taken a major backseat lately. I've never really had a "plan." I'm pretty certain I am done with reality TV, though. I've got two shows under my belt, and at this point I am enjoying a simpler life without a camera in my face. One thing factoring into my decision to leave the show is that this was supposed to be a show about my life, but I wanted to keep Jason and Palmer out of it. As a result of that contradiction, the show started to feel inauthentic. Other cast members gave more of their personal lives and it seemed hypocritical to keep mine private. I know being a mother will be my life's most important work, and I am finding more and more purpose in it every day.

Conclusion

WHAT YOU GAIN AS A MOM (BESIDES BABY WEIGHT)

Having kids feels like that first seventh-grade
crush that overwhelms every molecule in your
body, but it's permanent.

—KRISTEN BELL, MOTHER OF TWO

I know I've spent a lot of time un-painting the picture-perfect message of motherhood that appears on social media and blogs. Before I got pregnant, I worried about what I'd lose by having a child, and I was right that it wouldn't be smooth sailing. But what I did NOT realize was how much I would gain besides my beautiful baby girl. Do you want to expand your consciousness? Do you want to learn some life lessons? Well, a kid could help. The Native Americans believe that your children do not belong to you . . . they are lent to you by the Creator. They believe that they come to this earth as life's greatest teachers. This makes sense to me because Palmer is probably the most important teacher I've ever had. From the moment you get pregnant, you start learning how much you didn't know beforehand. Here are just a few things you gain:

Selflessness. You come face to face with the reality that it's no longer about you. I was a pretty selfish person before I had Palmer. And I'll admit that leading up to my pregnancy, I was kinda tired of myself and starting to feel a little self-absorbed. Well, y'all, that changes FAST, long before you even give birth. Pregnancy is when you have to start making decisions that are not only in *your* best interest, but also in the best interest of another human being— from what you're putting in your body to how much exercise you're doing to getting enough sleep. Palmer has pretty much slapped me in the face and said, "Look, bitch, it's not about you anymore." Don't get me started on the first night I was in the hospital, when the nurses woke me up every two hours to feed her. *Wait. What's happening here? I used to be able to sleep!* I used to be able to take long baths and pee by myself, too. But motherhood gets you out of your own head in a good way and forces you to have patience. You don't want to get up at 3 A.M. because the baby needs to be fed? Ha. Too bad.

The ability to see the world differently. Call it clichéd or cheesy or both, but having a child softened me. It has made me much more vulnerable, shown me the humanity in others and given me more empathy than ever for other people. Especially for single moms. My God, ladies, I BOW DOWN to you! Talk about the hardest job in the world. You will want your child to be a better human than you, and that's a good thing. Parenthood also pushes your limits. You want to be tough and ignore the GoFundMe asking for cancer treatment help for a three-year-old? Good luck . . . because you will imagine your own child in that position and want to give as much as you can.

Care and caution. I'm a worrier by nature, but being a mom has left me riddled with a new level of anxiety. I'm very accident prone and clumsy, and once I became a mother, I also got scared. God forbid something happens to me, I'm not going to be there for my child. (Oh, and I don't want Jason to remarry.) So I drive the speed limit like a little granny and I don't partake in dangerous activities like skiing. In fact, I've become super cautious about everything. I was a major germaphobe BEFORE coronavirus, so I keep sanitizing wipes in my purse and car at all times. I take much more calculated risks than I did before. When we went to Colorado on season six of *Southern Charm*, a party limo was scheduled to take us from the Denver airport to the Steamboat Springs ski resort. Having lived in Colorado, I knew this drive included long, winding roads and very steep mountain passes. It's scary enough in a regular car, so I couldn't believe we were going to attempt this in a party limo with NO seat belts. I flat-out refused to go unless they secured a safer vehicle, so they did. I'm such a buzzkill, I know.

An appreciation for the small moments. My first year of motherhood was one of the hardest times in my life. The expression "the days are long but the years are short" is so freaking true. I spent that first year trying so desperately to cling to my former identity. I was going to hire a nanny in an attempt to fully push myself back into my career. But I just kept thinking, *Why am I going to pay someone to do this when I realistically can do it myself?* At this point in her life, Palmer is growing and changing so quickly, I just don't want to miss anything. And I don't want to regret anything later. This time with my child is so precious and it's not time you get back, so I want to savor it.

The understanding that control is a mirage. I'm a control freak and I always have been. That therapist I saw before I got pregnant nailed it: my fear of getting pregnant spoke to my control-freak tendencies. Well, having a child teaches you that control is a mirage. I feel like having a child was a lesson presented to me by God, telling me that you have to learn to let go of some control. I'm learning or at least trying to embrace the idea that ultimately what's meant to be will be. When she was a baby, I spent a lot of time thinking, *What if something happens to Palmer? What would I do?* At one point, I thought about getting a nanny, but worrying about it literally kept me up at night. What if she put Palmer's diaper on too tight? What if she cut Palmer's food in too-big bites and she choked? Would the nanny know how to do the Heimlich maneuver? Would she know how to open the gate for the ambulance?

I shared this fear with my mom one day when she stopped by to visit.

"Everybody has those thoughts at some point, but they need to be fleeting little thoughts," she told me. "You cannot dwell on them or run with them. You need to get them out of your head as soon as you can." And since I know my mom is always right, I've really tried. After all, it's not healthy or a good use of my time.

Better priorities. Since becoming a mother, my priorities have changed. Among these top priorities are my true friendships. Throughout my life, I have met a LOT of people. I have had friendships come and go, of course, but at this station in my life I would rather have fewer quality friendships than lots of social acquaintances. I'm a hermit for the most part and I don't consider myself a socialite by any means. In my twenties I was much more of an extrovert, but as I've gotten older I would rather sit in a room with a few people or go to a one-on-one lunch than a big shindig or fundraiser. (I *loathe* schmoozing.) *Especially* since becoming a mama, I want my friendships to be of quality. I want to be around people I can relate to and who fill my tank instead of those people who I call energy vampires, the ones who make you feel like your spirit is being sucked dry when you're around them.

I have a couple of friends in their seventies that I go to lunch with and friends ten years younger than me, too. I have friends from all socioeconomic backgrounds and belief systems. I am also incredibly lucky to still have the core group of girlfriends that I have known since about the first grade. These are the girls who knew me long before I ever went on reality TV. They have been there through it all and we have always stuck together. We share the common bond of growing up in a small town and no matter how much time passes without seeing each other, we always pick up right where we left off. I call this group of girls my "solid gold friends." We will ALWAYS be there for one another, and I consider myself very fortunate to have such long-lasting friendships. The two things in common in all of my friendships are that they inspire me and/or make me laugh. I also want to be able to learn from the people I'm friends with.

A new love for your partner. Seeing Jason as a father has been one of the greatest joys of my life. If you question a man's ability to be a good dad, don't marry him. Seriously. I never once had any doubts that Jason would be a good father. I think every man secretly hopes for a son, whether he admits it or not. Jason grew up as one of three brothers and has five nephews and one niece. Needless to say, he knows boys better than girls. Jason is also a guy's guy. He hunts. He fishes. He likes fast cars and heavy machinery. When he first found out he was having a girl, I could tell he was a little nervous. That has all changed. He has flourished in his role as a girl's dad. When Palmer was about a year old, he admitted that he was actually glad we had a girl instead of a boy. He said, "Cam, I can't believe it, but being the dad of a girl has forced me to get out of my comfort zone and learn so much."

He treats Palmer with such patience and admiration. He is definitely the softy of the two of us. Palmer is a daddy's girl ALL the WAY. She WORSHIPS Jason. I'm a second thought once he gets home from work. (Yes, I'm salty about this, but it still warms my heart.) Jason is constantly teaching her things, showing her things. Whereas I will stick her in front of the TV sometimes while I get a chore done, Jason will actually involve her in the things that he does. (Yes . . . I can learn from him.) One time I came home and my eighteen-month-old was outside waxing a car in the driveway with him. He takes her on evening kayak rides, on trips to Home Depot, to the movies and on countless other adventures. He dances in the kitchen with her and lets her help when he bakes banana bread. (Yes, he bakes . . . I know, I don't deserve him.)

When Palmer was a year and a half old, I took her to Field and Stream and let her pick out her very own first fishing rod. I knew that being able to fish with his child was a dream of Jason's, so I thought it would be a fun surprise. She picked out a purple training rod with Elsa from the movie *Frozen* on it and a pink tackle box. Jason's eyes lit up when he saw it and he told Palmer he couldn't wait to take her fishing. They have not successfully caught a fish yet, but that doesn't matter. I know they will someday. It's more about the time they spend together and Jason being able to teach Palmer about something he loves to do.

Jason is also not of the old-school mentality that it's mostly the woman's job to take care of the child. He will work a long day in the hospital and still come home and give Palmer a bath and put her to bed. He shares in our responsibility equally and respects and honors the fact that I spend the majority of my time with her. He gives me a break when I need it and doesn't resent me for it. He is an extremely involved parent. I count my lucky stars that he is my husband, and these are all things I'd never have known about him without Palmer.

The chance to work on your marriage. Yes, marriage will inevitably change to some degree when you become a parent. (If you say yours remains unaffected, you are either lying or just very lucky.) Children bring a whole new set of stressful situations and worries. You are tired. You are worn thin. You don't have much time to yourselves. When it's just the two of you, you have a lot more freedom and the ability to be spontaneous. Before Palmer, Jason and I would go on at least two dates a week and now we are lucky if we get one every two months, and I can't tell you the last time we went on a vacation that was just the two of us. We also argue more now that we have a child. Sometimes I feel resentment toward Jason because he still leaves the house and goes to work every day. He gets to be around adults and have conversations while I am at home with a two-year-old. Yes, I know that it is an absolute privilege to even have this ability and I'm grateful for it, but it doesn't change the fact that sometimes the grass looks greener on the other side. (News flash: You are allowed to love being home with your child while sometimes hating it, too. That's NORMAL.) Sometimes when Jason comes home, I immediately want to just leave to have some alone time. He allows me to do this, bless his heart. I have my opinions on how things should be done and so does he. Of course, I always think I know best because I birthed Palmer—*ha!*—but we also respect each other even more now. We try to set a good example for Palmer and if we do have a heated argument, we don't do it around her. We try to show affection in front of her so she knows her parents love each other. Marriage is work 100 percent, and when you have a child it really shows you what a priority that work needs to be.

There are so many other lessons I've learned and things I've gained from becoming a mom, and I know with each age and stage, the list will continue to grow. All I can say is that having a baby was the hardest and best decision I ever made. Parenthood shows you this all-encompassing, truly unconditional love that you never knew existed. If you want to go on a spiritual journey, just have a kid. You will grow in more ways than you can imagine, and isn't that the whole point of life? I mean, if you're not learning and growing, what are you doing here?

There's a John Lennon quote I love that says, "Everything will be okay in the end. If it's not okay, it's not the end." It's so true, and children make this even clearer. A perfect analogy for this is the time I took Palmer to the Little Gym at five months old. As soon as I sat her down, to my horror, she started licking the floor. Moral of the story is . . . she lived. So y'all, just feed them and love them and they will be okay.

ACKNOWLEDGMENTS

One Day You'll Thank Me has been a labor of love to write. I would like to acknowledge several people who have helped make this book possible.

I would like to thank my husband, Jason, who is the rock in my life. I can't believe I tricked you into marrying me! Thank you for your unwavering support and love. You mean the world to me and are the best person I know.

To my daughter, Palmer, you are and will always be my sunshine. I am privileged that you chose me to be your mama and I love you with every fiber of my being. Your effervescence puts a smile on my face every day. I can't wait to see what all you become!

To my parents, thank you for always encouraging me to not be afraid of trying new things. You both have instilled values in me that I will always be grateful for.

To my sister, Cayce, God surely blessed me when he gave me you as a sister. I will always be in awe of your kind heart and open mind. I love you forever and always.

I would also like to acknowledge my team, who have encouraged this book with great enthusiasm. Thank you to Michele Bender for your guidance and warm heart; to Cait Hoyt, my literary agent at CAA, for your push to get me writing; to my manager, Antranig Balian, for always having my back; and to my commercial agent at CAA, Rick Lucas, for opening many doors for me.

Lastly, thank you to Natasha Simons at Gallery Books for making this book a reality and believing in me, and Maggie Loughran for her keen insight, as well as publisher Jennifer Bergstrom, associate publisher Jennifer Long, publicist Michelle Podberezniak, marketing director Abby Zidle, senior production editor Alysha Bullock, art directors Lisa Litwack and John Vairo, and interior designer Jaime Putorti, as well as the whole Gallery team.